Portrait of the Festiniog

Portread O Rheilffordd Ffestiniog

Portrait of the Festiniog

Portread O Rheilffordd Ffestiniog

Peter Johnson

IAN ALLAN
Publishing

First published 1992

ISBN 0 7110 2051 5

Published by Ian Allan Ltd, Shepperton, Surrey; and printed by Ian Allan Printing Ltd at their works at Coombelands in Runnymede, England.

Below:
The FR's deviation was an example of what could be achieved using the right motivation. Here we see *Mountaineer* at the head of a down train, whilst *Earl of Merioneth* heads across the bridge on the sprial bound for Blaenau Ffestiniog on 26 August 1986. *P. Q. Treloar*

Contents

Introduction

The Festiniog is a notable railway, for a narrow-gauge line: notable for its gradients, its early use of steam traction on passenger services, its adoption of the Fairlie locomotives. It is also remarkable for its ability to build its own locomotives and rolling stock, for its closure and revival, for its deviation spiral at Dduallt and for being the oldest unamalgamated railway company in the world, to name but a few of its attributes.

Without doubt the Festiniog Railway is also a line of contrasts: the estuaries of the Glaslyn and the Dwyryd; the artificial lakes of Llyn Mair and Llyn Ystradau; the woodland above Cei Mawr and the moorland around the Moelwyn Tunnel; the urban areas of Penrhyndeudraeth and Tany-grisiau, not to mention Blaenau Ffestiniog; the bustle of Harbour station and solitude of Dduallt. On the locomotive front, contrast the Festiniog's famous Fairlies with the equally famous England locomotives. Or compare the carriages, the vintage four-wheelers (the oldest such in regular use in the world?) with bang up-to-date centrally-heated bogie stock.

The Festiniog has always had a fascination for both tourist and enthusiast and its story has often been told — although not always as accurately as it should have been. Indeed, within 30 years of its opening the Board of Trade Inspector, Capt Henry Tyler, was extolling the line's virtues to the Institution of Civil Engineers and giving George England exclusive credit for the first locomotive design, thereby overlooking C. M. Holland's participation. (The impression is given that the Captain was actually using the FR as a vehicle to promote himself as an expert on narrow gauge railways in order to solicit consultancy commissions.) Within the limits of this volume it is not possible to go into the FR's story in great depth, but rather to paint a picture, a pen portrait if you will, which shows something of the best known

Below:
A *Prince*-hauled passenger train crossing the Cob, bound for Penrhyn, in 1957, shortly after car No 11 (left) had been turned for working with No 12 (centre); the latter had been provided with a buffet counter and provided with a corridor connection to the former.
Peter Treloar

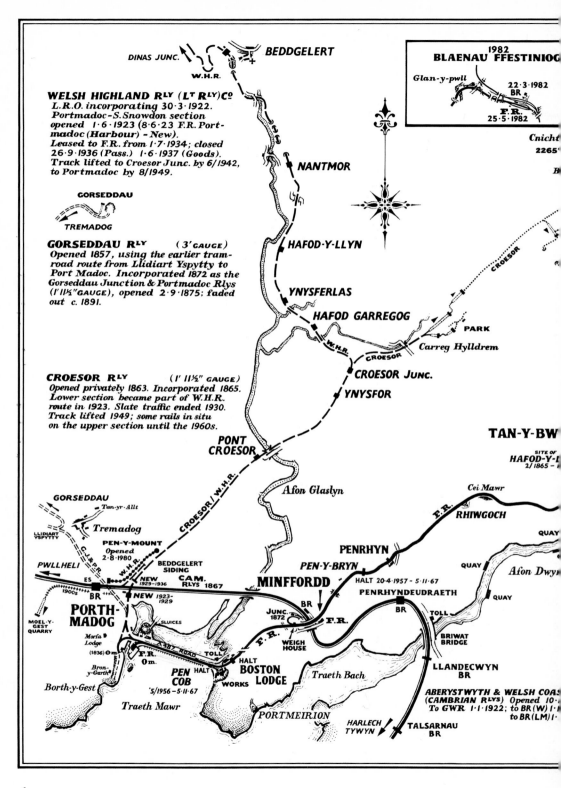

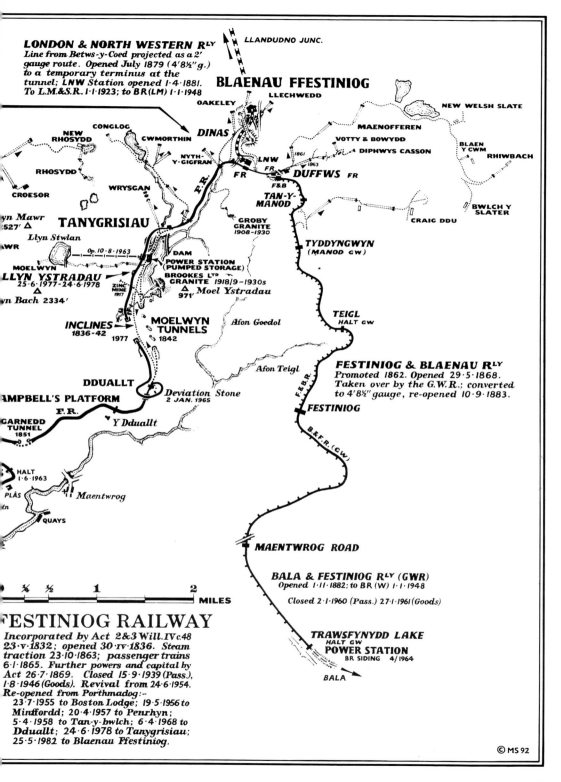

LONDON & NORTH WESTERN R^LY
Line from Betws-y-Coed projected as a 2'
gauge route. Opened July 1879 (4'8½"g.)
to a temporary terminus at the
tunnel; LNW Station opened 1·4·1881.
To L.M.&S.R. 1·1·1923; to BR(LM) 1·1·1948

LLANDUDNO JUNC.

BLAENAU FFESTINIOG

LLECHWEDD

OAKELEY

NEW WELSH SLATE

CONGLOG

NEW RHOSYDD

CWMORTHIN

DINAS

MAENOFFEREN

VOTTY & BOWYDD

BLAEN Y CWM

NYTH-Y-GIGFRAN

DIPHWYS CASSON

RHIWBACH

RHOSYDD

LNW

DUFFWS FR

1861

1863

FR

FR

CROESOR

WRYSGAN

F&B

TAN-Y-MANOD

BWLCH Y SLATER

yn Mawr
527' △

TANYGRISIAU

GROBY GRANITE 1908-1930

CRAIG DDU

Llyn Stwlan

Op. 10·8·1963

TYDDYNGWYN (MANOD GW)

AWR

MOELWYN

LLYN YSTRADAU
25·6·1977-24·6·1978

DAM

POWER STATION (PUMPED STORAGE)

BROOKES L^TD GRANITE 1918/9-1930s

ZINC MINE 1917

△ 971' Moel Ystradau

yn Bach 2334'

INCLINES
1836-42

1977

MOELWYN TUNNELS

1842

Afon Goedol

TEIGL HALT GW

FESTINIOG & BLAENAU R^LY
Promoted 1862. Opened 29·5·1868.
Taken over by the G.W.R.; converted
to 4'8½" gauge, re-opened 10·9·1883.

Afon Teigl

DDUALLT

Deviation Stone 2 JAN. 1965

FESTINIOG

AMPBELL'S PLATFORM

F.R.

Y Dduallt

B. & F.R. (GW)

GARNEDD TUNNEL 1851

HALT 1·6·1963

PLÀS

Maentwrog

MAENTWROG ROAD

QUAYS

BALA & FESTINIOG R^LY (GWR)
Opened 1·11·1882; to BR(W) 1·1·1948

Closed 2·1·1960 (Pass.) 27·1·1961 (Goods)

¼ ½ 1 2
MILES

FESTINIOG RAILWAY
Incorporated by Act 2&3 Will. IV c.48
23·v·1832; opened 30·IV·1836. Steam
traction 23·10·1863; passenger trains
6·1·1865. Further powers and capital by
Act 26·7·1869. Closed 15·9·1939 (Pass.),
1·8·1946 (Goods). Revival from 24·6·1954.
Re-opened from Porthmadog:-
23·7·1955 to Boston Lodge; 19·5·1956 to
Minffordd; 20·4·1957 to Penrhyn;
5·4·1958 to Tan-y-bwlch; 6·4·1968 to
Dduallt; 24·6·1978 to Tanygrisiau;
25·5·1982 to Blaenau Ffestiniog.

TRAWSFYNYDD LAKE HALT GW
POWER STATION
BR SIDING 4/1964

BALA

© MS 92

and most influential narrow gauge railway in the world.

The portrait, then, will draw attention to some of the Festiniog Railway's contrasts and its development since 1836. The story which *is* told is supported by some documentation which directs attention to various aspects of railway management and operation. The contrasts are provided by the Railway's General Managers writing in 1890 and 1991, the Locomotive Superintendent writing during World War 1, a consultant writing after it and a quarryman telling of his experiences on the quarrymen's train. These give an insight into the operation of the railway which is not readily available to the observer, however enthusiastic he or she may be.

Whilst the emphasis here is historical, it has little to do with nostalgia and more to do with explaining how the Festiniog Railway came to be what it is today, its notability, its contrasts.

Above:
Blanche and *Prince* crossing Cei Mawr in August 1962 with a wide variety of stock. The view here has been severely restricted due to the growth of conifers during the 1970s and 1980s but in 1991, following a change of land ownership, some progress had been made in opening up the view again. *John Dobson*

Below left:
Merddin Emrys on the ledge above Llyn Mair, approaching Garnedd Tunnel, with the 11.45 service from Porthmadog on 1 June 1973. *John Scrace*

Below:
Earl of Merioneth bound for Porthmadog in May 1986 is pictured with a train which includes two 'Barns' (showing the louvre windows which were a feature of these cars when built), Buffet Car No 14, three steel-bodied cars and three vintage bogie cars bringing up the rear. The Red Star Parcels logo is painted on the brake van door. *Norman Gurley*

Photographs

Photographically the Railway has been extensively covered since the 1870s. That said, there are gaps in known coverage — only one photograph is reported taken of the original *Mountaineer*, and that only exists as a magazine reproduction (*The Locomotive* Vol 26). New photographs do turn up from time to time, however, and one of the oldest known of the railway came into the company's possession within the last five years. The largest source of 19th century photographs are those taken by R. H. Bleasdale of Birmingham in 1887, many of which were included in the collection called the *Spooner Album*, now in the company's archives; the 44 Festiniog photographs listed in Bleasdale's catalogue have all been identified and some are reproduced here — Bleasdale sold a set of 44 12in x 15in prints, mounted or unmounted, for £6 12s 0d (£6.60), otherwise they were 4/- (20p) mounted or 3/6d (17.5p) unmounted. Recently a number of photographs taken around Portmadoc Harbour in the 1890s have come to light in the possession of Kirklees Metropolitan Council, in Yorkshire, and have proved to be of great interest and value; one of them is included here.

In the first years of the 20th century the pre-eminence of the picture postcard has provided rich pickings, supplying several views being published here for the first time in book form. Before World War 2 the development and increased availability of the hand-held camera allowed enthusiasts to make extensive photographic records, although almost none were allowed in Boston Lodge Works; examples of this work are also to be found within. These, together with views showing the Festiniog Railway since restoration commenced and as it is in the 1990s, provide further contrasts. Whilst many facets of the railway are illustrated, regrettably there are many others which are not: signalling, telephones, track, the Ffestiniog & Blaenau, the quarries, to name just a few.

Indeed, as always, many more photographs were considered for publication and rejected than it has been possible to include.

Below:
Dinas Junction in 1887 with a train of assorted wagons and one of the larger England locomotives on the line from Blaenau Ffestiniog; a gunpowder van, presumably empty, is next to the locomotive. Considerable changes took place in this area after the line at the foot of the mountain became swamped with slate waste. Glan-y-pwll signal box is on the right. *R. H. Bleasdale*

Acknowledgements

Publication of this book will nearly coincide with the 21st anniversary of my first acquaintance with the Festiniog Railway, so I would like to take this opportunity to express my thanks to all those who have supplied me with photographs and information regarding the railway over the years, and to those who have made photographs possible.

This time I have particularly enjoyed the support of Adrian Gray (who is compiling an archive of prewar FR photographs for the Festiniog Railway Heritage Group), John Alsop, Ernie Dunsford, Gillian Goddard, Norman Gurley, Paul Ingham, Peter Jarvis, David Pollock, Howard Rôbins, Gill Shephard, F. W. (Tim) Shuttleworth, Rodney Weaver, Keeli White and Ffestin Williams. The Company's archivist provided a level of service we have all come to expect. I have also enjoyed revisiting the National Library of Wales at Aberystwyth and the Dolgellau and Caernarfon offices of the Gwynedd County Council's Archives Department.

Special thanks are also due to those who have contributed to the Festiniog Railway *Magazine* (of which I have the honour to be editor), both as contributors and as participants in the events recorded therein; without them my task would have been a great deal more difficult. I would also like to pay tribute to my predecessors and colleagues on the *Magazine*, Dan Wilson and Norman Gurley, for it was the *Magazine* they produced which encouraged me to want to know this finest of narrow gauge railways better.

In his IMechE paper, David Pollock acknowledges the contributions of John Routly, Jon Whalley, Bob McGregor, Brian Bushell, Norman Gurley, Phil Girdlestone, Steve McCullum and the Company's archivist.

Any opinions offered are my own and not those of the Festiniog Railway Company or the Festiniog Railway Society Ltd. Equally, I accept full responsibility for any errors I may have perpetrated and perpetuated.

Readers who would like to join me in contributing to the '*Taliesin* 2000' scheme for building a replica single Fairlie can obtain further details by sending a self-addressed stamped envelope to A. J. Savage, c/o Festiniog Railway Co, Porthmadog, Gwynedd LL49 9NF.

Those who would like to add to Adrian Gray's prewar photographic archive should write to him c/o Harbour Station. One picture or 100, all are welcome, as are both enthusiasts' work and holiday snaps.

A list of 4mm and 7mm drawings of FR locomotives and rolling stock is available from Harbour station, on receipt of a stamped, self-addressed envelope.

Finally, those who would like details of my postcard research, or who might be able to add to it, should write to 12 Maplewell Drive, Leicester LE4 1BD.

Peter Johnson
Leicester
January 1992

Placenames and Spellings

In its 1832 Act of Parliament the company's name was spelled Festiniog; the first Welsh dictionary, standardising the language, was published over 30 years later. It is now considered that 'The Festiniog Railway Company' is the correct legal form. In recent years the company has adopted the form 'Ffestiniog Railway', and the Welsh equivalent, 'Rheilffordd Ffestiniog', in its marketing.

Many Welsh place names have changed over the years, especially since the 1960s as Welsh has become increasingly predominant over English. The earlier forms are used when quoting and no attempt has been made to standardise elsewhere.

Origins and Expansion

The Festiniog Railway Company gained its Act of Incorporation in 1832 and opened its line between Portmadoc and Blaenau Ffestiniog in 1836. It was built to carry slate from the quarries at Blaenau Ffestiniog to the harbour at Portmadoc — including the branches to Dinas and Duffws at Blaenau — a distance of just under 14 miles.

Blaenau Ffestiniog slate was (and is) of good quality and much in demand. The demand could only be met with difficulty, due to limitations of transport locally. At the quarries dressed slate was first loaded onto the backs of pack animals. By this means it was carried to quays on the banks of the Afon Dwyryd, at or below Maentwrog. There it was trans-shipped to river-going craft for

Above:
In August 1989, *Merddin Emrys* near Gelli Wiog on the deviation line with tourist cars next to the locomotive.
Norman Gurley

Right:
A regular feature of Festiniog operations from the late 1980s, although not permanently in the timetable, is the vintage train operation. Run for a variety of reasons, a vintage train will consist totally of 19th century motive power and rolling stock, and usually includes four-wheelers as well as bogie vehicles; often photo-stops and run-pasts are arranged, too. On 17 June 1990 a train was run for guests of the FR Society from other railways; at Dduallt Tank Curve, the *Prince*-hauled train comprised van No 2 of 1885, 'Bug Box' No 5 of 1863, Brown, Marshalls Nos 15 and 16 of 1872 and Nos 12 and 11 built by the Gloucester Wagon Co in 1880. *Author*

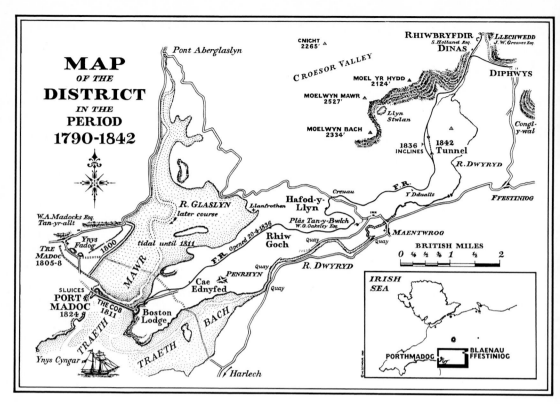

MAP
OF THE
DISTRICT
IN THE
PERIOD
1790-1842

Pont Aberglaslyn

CNICHT
2265'

CROESOR VALLEY

RHIWBRYFDIR
S.Holland Esq.
DINAS

LLECHWEDD
J.W.Greaves Esq.

DIPHWYS

MOEL YR HYDD
2124'

MOELWYN MAWR
2527'

Llyn
Stwlan

Congl-
y-wal

MOELWYN BACH
2334'

1836
INCLINES

1842
Tunnel

R.DWYRYD

R. GLASLYN
later course

Llanfrothen

Hafod-y-
Llyn

Creuau

F.R.

Y Dduallt

FFESTINIOG

W.A.Madocks Esq.
Tan-yr-allt

Plâs Tan-y-Bwlch
W.O.Oakeley Esq.

INN

MAENTWROG

Ynys
Fadog

1800

tidal until 1811

F.R. Opened 20·4·1836

Rhiw
Goch

Quay

Quay

BRITISH MILES
0   ¼ ½ ¾ 1   ½   2

TRE
MADOC
1805-8

Quay

PENRHYN

R. DWYRYD

IRISH
SEA

SLUICES
PORT
MADOC
1824

THE COB
1811

Boston
Lodge

Cae
Ednyfed

Quay

Ynys Cyngar

TRAETH

TRAETH BACH

MAWR

PORTHMADOG

BLAENAU
FFESTINIOG

Harlech

the journey to the sea. There, at sea and close to what later became Portmadoc, it was trans-shipped again, to larger coastal craft for carriage to its ultimate destination. This repeated loading and unloading, with consequent damage to the goods, was extremely expensive. The railway was proposed to reduce costs.

A narrow gauge of 1ft 11½in was adopted and the line was designed to have a continuous falling gradient down to the harbour so that laden trains could be worked down by gravity; horses pulled the empty wagons back up the hill. The last mile to Portmadoc utilised Madocks's 1811 embankment across the Glaslyn estuary. James Spooner, the railway's engineer, skilfully adapted the continuous gradient to the contours, putting the railway onto some exposed ledges and round numerous curves. The sharpest of these is called Tyler's after the Board of Trade Inspecting Officer. Where the contours were unsuitable some imposing dry-stone embank-

ments were built; the highest, at Cei Mawr, is 62ft high. To improve the route the Moelwyn Tunnel (730yd) was opened in 1842, followed by the Garnedd Tunnel (60yd) in 1851; the length and narrow bore of the former, combined with a lack of ventilation, were to result in the railway achieving a certain notoriety, especially when the 20th century's interwar years brought an increasing number of tourists as passengers.

Right:
Sometimes the slate empties were taken up on their own as seen here at Tanygrisiau. The power station access road follows a line close to that occupied by the train in this prewar picture; the deviation route runs behind the house. *Author's Collection*

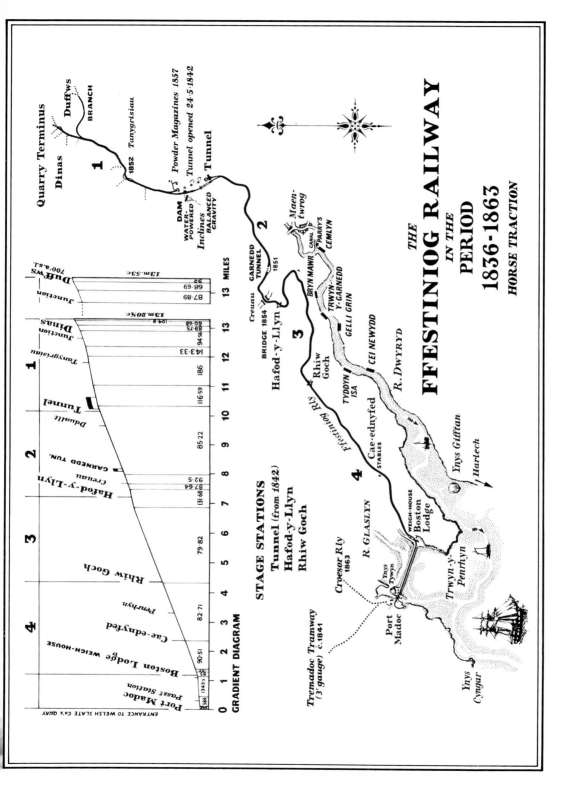

THE FEESTINIOG RAILWAY

IN THE PERIOD 1836-1863

HORSE TRACTION

STAGE STATIONS

Tunnel (from 1842)
Hafod-y-Llyn
Rhiw Goch

GRADIENT DIAGRAM

ENTRANCE TO WELSH SLATE Co's QUAY

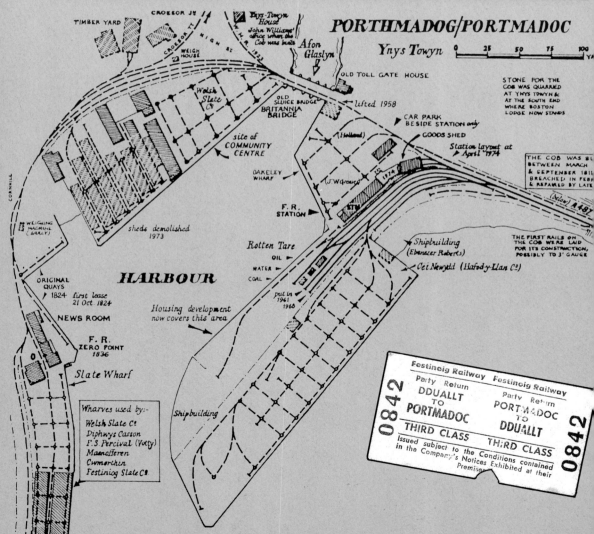

STATIONS
Portmadoc

Left:
The stone station building at Portmadoc was built in 1879; its position, and that of the contemporary goods shed, were the reverse of the structures they replaced. The photographer has captured the scale of the station, as well as the track gang working on the siding and the England loco shunting the goods shed. *Commercial postcard — Lloyd & Son*

Right:
Harbour station had no access from the back, now the car park side, until 1960. Along the front, from the right, the doors were for the: ladies' waiting room (and lavatory); booking office; waiting room; office, station master's flat (ground floor) and office and board room (upstairs); coal store; porters' room. *Author's Collection*

Above:
By 30 July 1971 a number of changes had been made. The first floor had become the General Manager's flat; the gents had moved into the coal store, paid for by the CEGB; the dormer window marked the location of the Control Office and the window in the end gable, the sales store. A small shop and a tea-bar had been installed in the booking hall and a museum established in the old waiting room. *Merddin Emrys* is seen arriving with a train which includes Buffet Car No 14, which was built from ex-Lynton & Barnstaple Railway carriage components. *Linda* waits to take the train out as the 13.15 departure. *P. H. Groom*

Boston Lodge Works

Above:

Boston Lodge Works in 1887. From the left the buildings were cottages, still occupied, which were originally stabling during the construction of the Cob; carpenters' shop, now stores building; carpenters' saw mill —the white building — which was demolished in 1956 and its site now occupied by a mess block; the engine house, with chimney and pattern loft above, now machine shops and offices; and, 'erecting shed', built for construction of *Merddin Emrys*. Rolling stock includes a coal wagon, timber and iron framed slate wagons and *The Princess*.

R. H. Bleasdale

BOSTON LODGE

25   50   YDS

TURNTABLE
built 1869
out of use 1923

MINFF

removed 1944

ORIGINAL WEIGH-HOUSE
(HOSTEL)

SITE OF 1923 HALT
Boston Lodge for Portme

former
OIL STORE
S&T STORES

Boston Lodge Halt
opened 23·7·1955

LOCO SHED
ROW USED
AS Carriage
Shed

WATER TANK

WORKS ROAD ACCESS

SAND PIT

LAYOUT
AT APRIL 1974

OFFICE

ORIGINAL
WAGON SHOP

OFFICE

derelict

GATE

ROAD
TOLL GATE

rock face

TURNOUT
8/1973

GATE
removed
APR. 1971

KEY

USES FROM 1866 &
LATER RECORDS

FROM
1969

1 { Nº1 BOSTON LODGE
2 { Nº2 BOSTON LODGE
3 { COAL DEPOT; S. & T.
   { LATER OIL STORES
4 JOINERS' SHOP demolis
5 SMITHY
5 FOUNDRY
7 { ENGINE HOUSE
   { & BOILER
8 { SMITHY/BRASS
9 { ENGINE HOUSE
   { ('MODEL ROOM' OVER)
10 ERECTING SHOP
11 { CARPENTERS
   { SAW MILL
12 { CARPENTERS' SHOP
   { later OFFICE/STORES & S
13 PAINT SHOP
14 CARRIAGE SHED

CARRIAGE
PIT
to 1946

demolished
1962

layout
altered 1968

LOCO PIT

PEN COB HALT (cl 5·11·1967)

COB

SIGNAL BOX

lifted
1962

LOCO PIT

layout
altered
1962, 1965, 1973

Crane
base

demolished
1956

ASH
TIP

*Glan-y-Mor
Yard*

layout
altered
1962, 1965, 1973

Powder Magazines

16

Right:
The interior of Carnforth-built car No 112, during finishing and fitting out in the Glan-y-mor car shops during May 1991. A central heating radiator runs along the side, under the seats; the heating boiler and gas compartment is in the right hand corner. Seats of this type are being fitted to some of the older steel-bodied cars. *Author*

Below:
The erecting shop interior in 1931. In the foreground is *Merddin Emrys* with a power bogie removed — no doubt the present day safety officer would be very impressed with the support! Behind is the then newly repaired boiler for *Livingston Thompson* which had been sent away in 1929. *Merddin Emrys* was to remain out of use until 1934, whilst *Livingston Thompson* was to return to traffic, as *Taliesin*, later in 1931. *R. G. Jarvis*

Locomotives and Gravity

As a gravity line the railway worked very well, until the quarries' output was threatened with delay caused by a wagon shortage; unloading time at the harbour combined with the length of time taken to return an ever-increasing number of wagons back to the quarries caused the quarry owners to exert pressure on the railway's directors to increase its capacity. (It has to be said that some of the difficulties with the railway-owned wagons was caused by the quarries' using them

for their own purposes and keeping them out of circulation.) An increase in horse power could not be considered as already up to four animals were needed for each train of approximately 30 wagons. In 1856 it took more than five hours for the empties to complete their journey back to the quarries, while a train of slates took 92min to descend the line. Coincidentally, the directors had become concerned about the increasing cost of horse traction and, additionally, there could be

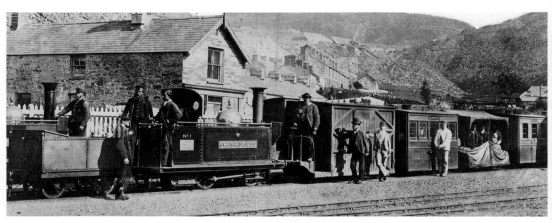

no possibility of the FR being allowed to carry passengers under these circumstances. An alternative would have to be found.

In the 1830s the use of steam traction on a railway such as the Festiniog was not a serious proposition; it barely made the grade on the standard gauge, never mind the narrow. But, as

ENGLAND LOCOMOTIVES
Princess
Above left:
Princess, slightly modified from it original condition, stands at Duffws. A tool box has been installed in the tender, which is clearly a different colour to the locomotive. The name was shortened when the locomotive was rebuilt in 1895. Behind the tender can be seen the top of the front end of *Palmerston,* the closest this locomotive came to being photographed in original condition. *Real Photos*

Left:
From 1969 to 1980, apart from a visit to Shildon for the Stockton & Darlington Railway 150th anniversary celebrations in 1975, *Princess* was on outside display in Blaenau Ffestiniog. It is shown in Boston Lodge Works being prepared for display in the Harbour Station Museum, its home since April 1981. *Author*

Above:
The Harbour Station Museum underwent some layout modifications in 1990, when it was made more accessible, and *Princess* was given a more prominent position. Other relics include a horse dandy wagon, wooden slate wagon and the hearse van. Photographed on 16 June 1990. *Author*

with all new technologies, developments and improvements were made as time passed. It was in 1860 that the FR Company Board decided to take action when it instructed the Secretary, Charles Easton Spooner (who had in 1856 also succeeded his father as engineer), to investigate the possibility of using steam engines on the line, examining as he did so, the locomotives already at work on the 2ft 7½in gauge Neath Abbey Ironworks line in South Wales. He was also to consult with Charles Menzies Holland, a young engineer being promoted by his uncle, Samuel Holland, the railway's first quarry customer.

The requirement was for a locomotive weighing not more than five tons (later increased to eight tons), having a low centre of gravity, capable of running up-hill (on a ruling grade of 1 in 79) at 8mph and downhill without a train (which

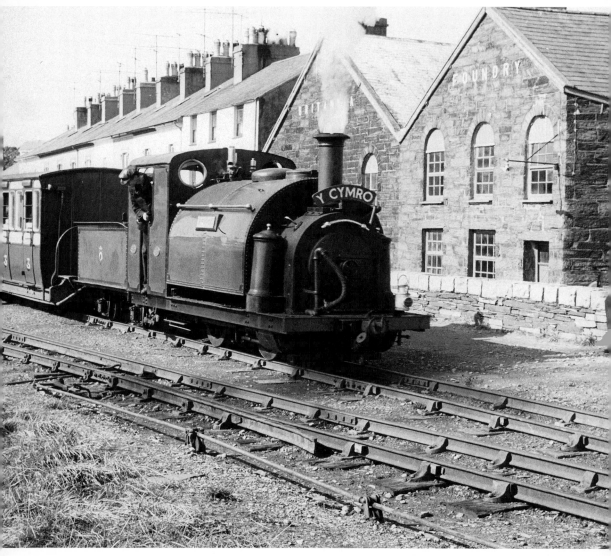

Prince

Left:
Photographed in 1887, *Prince* was named as shown until it was rebuilt in 1891. Here, saddle-tank-shaped weights have been added to the tops of the side-tanks and boiler to improve adhesion. *R. H. Bleasdale*

Below left:
Prince is seen leaving Portmadoc with 'Y Cymro' ('The Welshman'), the non-stop for Tan-y-bwlch, in 1964. During the 1955 rebuild the frames were modified as shown. *R. G. Rees*

Palmerston

Above right:
Palmerston is pictured shunting stock at Harbour station between the wars. The cylindrical objects alongside the smokeboxes of these locomotives carried sand. *Author's Collection*

Right:
Last used to power a steam hammer in Boston Lodge Works during World War 2, the restoration of *Palmerston* was for many years considered an impossibility; a Society 1960 AGM-day prank suggests that not everyone rated it as a valuable relic. *John Alexander*

Below:
Sold for private restoration in 1974, *Palmerston* returned to the Railway for the work to be completed in 1987. Photographed during the FR 'Steam 125' gala in 1988, the positioning conceals the absence of a boiler. Restoration as a coal-fired locomotive will make rapid progress following the installation of the new boiler built in 1991. *Author*

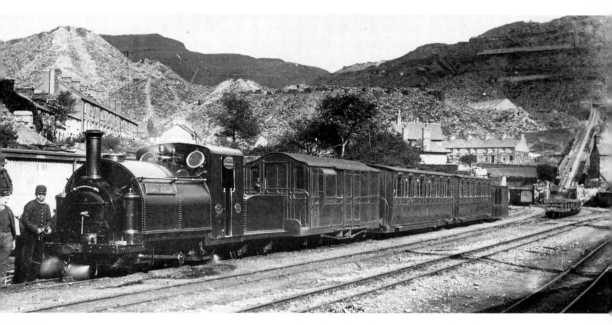

Welsh Pony

Above left:
Welsh Pony, substantially rebuilt, at the original Harbour station, c1871. The carriages are, in order from the locomotive, 3rd class, 1st class, open, Boston Lodge-built brake. The similarity of components of the station building to those at Penrhyn can easily be seen in this photograph. *FR Archives*

Left:
Since 1985 *Welsh Pony* has been on display by the entrance to Harbour station, performing a promotional purpose and being an attraction for children, and others, who like to climb on it. Since coming under the care of the Railway's Parks & Gardens Department the locomotive has been painted in historical livery and replica nameplates have been provided in English and in Welsh. *Author*

Little Giant

Above:
Little Giant at Duffws with a passenger train sometime after its 1888 rebuild. The curly-top brake van was one of three built in 1873 and 1876, one was given a new body in 1921 and became No 10; this has been recently restored. *Collection R. E. Tustin*

would continue to work by gravity) at 10mph. Several designs were considered, some of a most peculiar nature, including a strange six-coupled machine of Holland's design which would probably have done itself a terminal injury had it ever run. It was, however, recommended to the Board by Spooner and Holland and by October 1862 specifications had been drawn up and blueprints

made. An advertisement was placed in *The Engineer* inviting interested parties to tender for constructing three locomotives.

Despite having only 10 days in which to respond, the norm for those days, 29 firms declared an interest, although several backed off when they saw the specification! Of those who did make an offer, several also submitted their own designs or made criticisms of the FR's. Prices ranged from £565 to £1,869; calculations based on them showed that steam operation would be financially worthwhile. No offer was received from the Hatcham works of George England & Co.

Holland, being London-based, knew of George England and had already put him forward as a possible manufacturer for the FR; using England would facilitate liaison between the parties. England, however, was not keen on building one-offs or on re-arranging his construction techniques for short runs, so he did not respond to the invitation to tender.

While the tenders which had been received were being evaluated, Spooner and Holland opened negotiations with England. In February 1863 England agreed to 'make three small locomotive Engines' to Holland's design 'subject to any alterations that will be necessary'; the price was to be £900 each. The third engine was not to be delivered until the first two had been tried in traffic and was to incorporate any modifications found necessary. Within a short space of time England had persuaded Holland to see the error of his ways and a modified design of four-

23

coupled tank engine with an auxiliary coal-carrying tender was agreed upon (although not without some discussion, for the price was now £1,000 for the first two and £800 for the third); the first two locomotives were to be delivered by 1 June 1863. This deadline was not achieved but delivery did occur shortly afterwards, on 18 July. The engines were taken by rail to Caernarfon and then hauled overland, through Port Madoc, to Boston Lodge works.

For reasons as yet unexplained, four locomotives were delivered under the original contract. The first to arrive were *The Princess* (the first steamed) and *Mountaineer*. As might be expected, the first trials were not a success but by October 1863 a journalist from the North Wales *Chronicle* was cheerfully, and verbosely, reporting on the first public trip up the line on 23 October, observing two engines running at 10-12mph with a load of approximately 200 passengers, probably the first to be carried, although the regular passenger service was not commenced until 1865. Apparently the third locomotive, *The Prince*, was built in 1863, although not delivered until the following year, which also saw the construction and delivery of *Palmerston*; they cost £975 7s 6d each.

The effect on the FR was revolutionary. The whole method of operation of the railway was changed, and within a short time was recognisably the same as that which lasted until 1939. The England engines enabled the railway to cope with the ever-increasing slate traffic, although, as will be seen, they were not the final solution to the railway's capacity problems.

As built, the England engines were not exactly satisfactory, which is not surprising in view of their novelty. They lacked steam space, adhesive weight and water capacity, and were soon found to be too slow and rough-riding. Measures were taken to cure these faults and gradually the appearance of the engines evolved into the form which we all know. Two improved and enlarged members of the class were added in 1867, *Welsh Pony* and *Little Giant*, before the FR turned to more radical means to solve its motive power problems.

Despite their short reign as front-line power, it is gratifying to reflect that three of the first four locomotives have survived to the present day (*Mountaineer* was declared 'unroadworthy' in 1879 and scrapped) and that one of them is still earning its keep, even if in a condition which could never have been envisaged by its builders. The three survivors, and the also-extant *Welsh Pony*, must have earned their cost many times over, fully justifying the decision to dispense with horse power.

The introduction of steam traction did not bring about the end of gravity operation of loaded slate trains. The reason for its continued use on the Festiniog is explained by Major Spring, later; other gravity lines abandoned this method of working as soon as steam power was introduced. It is therefore of interest to look at the rules which governed the operation of the FR's gravity trains, especially as it is reported that they ran at speeds of up to 40mph without continuous or powered brakes! Though dated 1902, these rules represent working practices from 1836 to 1939:

FESTINIOG RAILWAY
SPECIAL RULES
for
Working Loaded Slate Trains
1 The greatest caution and vigilance must be observed by the Brakesmen working the loaded Slate Trains down the gradients.
2 The Brakes of every wagon must be carefully examined by the Brakesmen before starting and the brakes securely applied but not so as to skid the wheels. A wagon having a defective brake must be taken out and left on the siding.
3 The Brakesman must be careful to see that all the wagons in the train are properly coupled and under no circumstances must they start until this has been done.
4 The Slate Train from Rhiw must be brought to a stand on the Main Line below Glan-y-pwll Junction so as to be clear for the slate train from Duffws being connected to it. Sufficient brakes must be put down to do this.
5 The Slate train from Duffws must have the brakes pinned down so as to stop easily and smoothly to connect behind the Slate train from Rhiw.

CARRIAGES
Four-wheel carriages

Above right:
Third and first class four-wheel open cars photographed in 1887; it is likely that the cover on the third class vehicle was added at Boston Lodge. Built by Brown, Marshalls in 1863/64, these vehicles survive as Nos 7 and 6. *R. H. Bleasdale*

Right:
The first class open as seen on 3 June 1932, now with the 'observation car' appellation — which no doubt impressed those travelling in it through the Moelwyn Tunnel! *H. C. Casserley*

6 The Stationmaster at Duffws must ascertain the number of wagons from Rhiw and from Duffws and arrange that in no case shall a train be run without 2 Brakesmen in attendance. That with trains consisting of over 80 wagons there shall be 3 Brakesmen and that no train shall consist of more than 120 wagons in all. Only Brakesmen who are thoroughly experienced in the working of the Line are to be allowed to have charge of the trains. While having due regard to convenience of working the trains shall be so marshalled as to prevent the Brakesmen from having to travel an undue distance on a train between the braked wagons under their control.

7 The Head Brakesman must see that there is 1 braked wagon to every 5 unbraked wagons in the train before starting the train from Glan-y-pwll Junction.

8 Brakesmen are to be particularly careful when starting or stopping and also to so regulate their working when running as to prevent a breakage of wagon couplings or drawbars.

9 Brakesmen must keep a good look out on the running of their train and in case of a broken axle or wheel or any other defect the train must be brought to a stand and the wagon taken out. When one of the Brakesmen wants to draw the attention of the others he must blow his horn twice.

10 The Brakesmen must watch the trains while running down the line and if necessary must apply more brakes or tighten up those that have already been put down in order to keep the train under complete control and to bring it to a stand above the Weigh Office at Minffordd.

11 The Brakesmen must keep a sharp look out and be prepared to pay instant attention to the Signals on approaching the Glan-y-pwll Junction from Duffws and from Rhiw and in approaching the different Stations and Level Crossings along the Line. The Head Brakesman must give notice of the approach of his train by blowing his horn three times.

12 During the winter months a hanging lamp showing a white light must be fixed in front of the first wagon in the train and a red light behind the last wagon.

13 The Schedule time set forth in the time table for the Slate trains must be kept as near as possible and in no case must the speed be exceeded especially over the sharp curves.

14 The Head Brakesman is responsible that the train does not start from Glan-y-pwll Junction without the Staff or Ticket from the Signalman in charge of No 3 Box and that he gets the Staff or Ticket at the different Staff Stations on the way.

15 These Special Rules do not supersede the instructions in the Book of Rules and Regulations but are to be considered as an addition to the same.

J. S. Hughes
General Manager
Portmadoc, March 1st 1902

Extract from:
Rules and Regulations for the conduct of the traffic and for the guidance of the officers and men in the service of the Festiniog Railway Company (1872)

182 Every Guard and Brakesman is to see that his Signal lamps are in a fit state for use, and properly trimmed; the Guard in the rear of the Train must ascertain that the Tail Lamp is securely fixed before the Train starts; and is responsible for its being lighted at sunset as well as during fog.

203 The Brakesmen are prohibited from allowing any one to ride in the Brakesman's or slate wagons, or in the Train, without written authority; and any disobedience of this order will be punished.

204 Brakesmen are always to be very careful in getting between wagons to uncouple them, and are not to do so while the Train is in motion, except when specially ordered.

216 The Brakesman to arrange the brakes on every Train before starting down the line, by bracing them up in such a way that the Train can be controlled by two Brakesmen.

217 The chief Brakesmen are to keep a look out for every damage and injury done to the slate wagons, or trucks, and to keep a regular account in the books provided for them of every damage and injury that they might discover, and to note down, with the date of such damage, and description of how done and by whom, regularly and particularly given, and to submit a return or duplicate daily at the Head Office, and for the information of the Waggon Inspector at the Port. Any brakesman who shall be seen or found locking the break wheels by tightening the brake too much, and allowing the wheels to slide on the rails, will be liable to a fine or dismissal.

218 The Brakesman will take charge of every Down Slate Train, and run down the

line and keep the times as set out on the time table: in no case to run over the sharp curves at too great a speed.

219 To assist in taking any trucks, carriages, or wagons from the Train, at such places or Stations as they may be required to be left on the line, and also in running them into a turnout or shed as directed, and as per instructions of the Guard of the Train.

220 To be active, civil, generally useful and obliging, to lose no time in the discharge of their duties, and to be strictly honest and sober.

221 Should any Brakesman observe anything out of order in any of the carriages, wagons, or trucks, or anything else irregular or contrary to these Rules, or in any way injurious to the Company's property, he is immediately to acquaint the Guard of the Train, and the policeman on the line.

222 On arrival at the weighing office, to

Below:
The four-wheeled Brown, Marshalls stock was quickly brought back into use in 1958 to cope with increasing demand for travel to Tan-y-bwlch, which had been re-opened that year. A *Prince*-hauled train passes Boston Lodge on 5 June 1963 with Quarrymen's No 8 and Brown, Marshalls Nos 6, 5, 4 and 3, in that order. (These things were very important in those days.)
Norman Gurley

attend to the brakes in weighing the Trains, and to the instructions of the Guard of the Train, and to detach any truck out of order or damaged, which it may be necessary to send into the yard at Boston Lodge, leaving it in charge of the proper person.

223 These Rules are subject to such alterations as may be deemed advisable by the Directors.

224 Great attention is required as to 'Signals' and 'General Regulations'.

243 The Train Staff is to be carried on the Engine with all Up Trains; and with the Guard or Brakesman of the last part of every Down Train.

247 The Guard or Brakesman in charge of the last part of the Down Train is to carry the Train Staff, to indicate that nothing more is to follow.

The introduction of steam engines led the way to the carriage of passengers, a move encouraged by the threat of competing routes to Blaenau Ffestiniog. Using tiny four-wheeled carriages built in Birmingham, the first (official) passenger trains ran on 5 January 1865. The carriages had actually been obtained from Brown, Marshalls & Co early in 1864; the intervening time had been spent dealing with the requirements of the Board of Trade and its Inspecting Officer, Capt H. W. Tyler. Tyler did propose that the company think about introducing what we now know as bogie carriages; the first were introduced in January 1873.

Increasing traffic again brought operating problems which the company sought to solve by laying a second track. Parliamentary powers had been obtained in 1869 and the necessary land purchases put in hand when the problem was

Above left:
By 1885 this was state of the art for quarrymen's carriages. It seated 14 around the sides and on top of the brake cylinder. The photograph of No 8 (post-revival numbering) was taken in 1936. *G. F. Parker*

resolved at far less cost by the introduction of a locomotive capable of prodigious feats of haulage when compared with the existing fleet.

The saviour was *Little Wonder*, an articulated locomotive built, also in London, to Robert Fairlie's patent. Delivered in 1869, it was fitted with a double-ended boiler having twin fireboxes in the middle. The boiler was carried on two four-coupled power bogies which could swivel under it, the crew being carried one on either side of the fireboxes. The resulting machine was effectively twice the size of the original engines yet, being

19th CENTURY BOGIE STOCK

Above:
Cars Nos 15 and 16 are the doyens of the FR's 19th century bogie stock, being reckoned to be the first bogie carriages in regular service in the United Kingdom and the oldest of their type in regular service in the world. Both are, however, due for major works attention. No 16, shown here on 20 October 1991, was first restored in 1969. *Author*

articulated, was still well able to cope with the railway's bends and gradients. *Little Wonder* proved to be very successful, attracting attention from all over the world. The inventor gave the company free use of the patent and the double Fairlie became the Festiniog's trademark.

Having proved that bogies worked on a locomotive, the company then applied the same

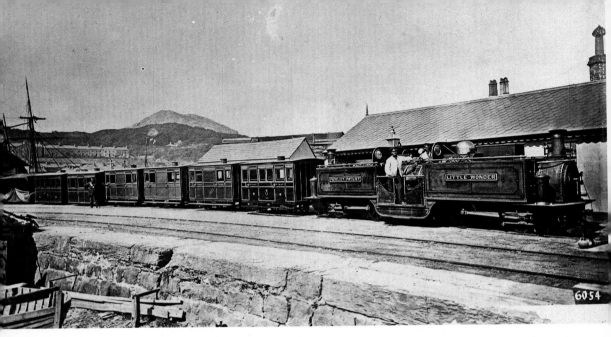

principle to its passenger stock in a move to increase both capacity and comfort. The year 1873 saw the introduction of two iron-framed bogie carriages, most likely the first of this type to run in the British Isles. These vehicles, Nos 15 and 16, are still in service. Built by Brown, Marshalls & Co of Birmingham, the carriage bodies have great strength due to their most unusual feature, not repeated in later Festiniog carriage construction — an integral wrought-iron frame.

FAIRLIE LOCOMOTIVES
Little Wonder

Above:
The first of the double Fairlies, *Little Wonder* is seen at the old Harbour station c1871. The locomotive was built by George England in 1869 and was condemned in 1882. The train shown here includes a variety of four-wheeled stock, including a first class coach next to the locomotive and an open car at the rear. It is thought that components of the original Harbour station were used later at Penrhyn. *Loco Pub Co*

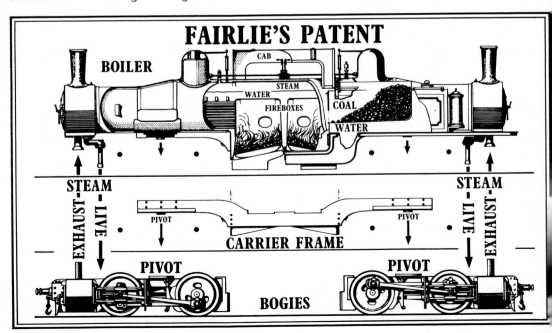

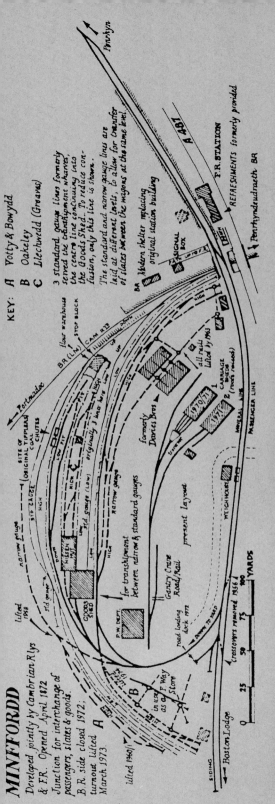

MINFFORDD

Developed jointly by Cambrian Rlys & F.R. Opened April 1872. Junction for interchange of passengers, slates & goods. B.R. side closed 1972. turnout lifted March 1973.

KEY:
A Votty & Bowydd
B Oakeley
C Llechwedd (Greaves)

3 standard gauge lines formerly served the transhipment wharves, the centre line continuing into the doods Shed. To reduce confusion, only this line is shown.

The standard and narrow gauge lines are laid at different levels, to allow for transfer of slates between the wagons at the same level.

BA Modern shelter replacing original station building

Minffordd

Below:

Minffordd in 1887. The train, hauled by *James Spooner*, includes both open four-wheelers, Nos 15 and 16 and a bogie luggage van. Refreshments were served from the lean-to building at the right. *R. H. Bleasdale*

Bottom:

Seen from above the ramp to the standard gauge station, this early 20th century view of Minffordd station was chosen by a local shopkeeper as representative of the locality. The England locomotive has a slate wagon containing three platform barrows in tow. The shelter on the down platform, of which this is the best known view, is thought to predate the stone building. *Commercial postcard — Wm Roderick, Minffordd*

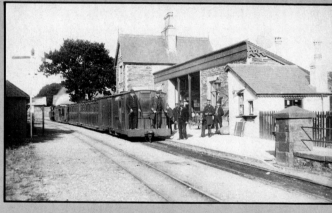

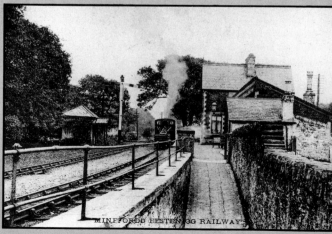

MINFFORDD FESTINIOG RAILWAY

31

Above:
After the railway closed in 1946 parts of the track quickly became overgrown, as illustrated here in 1948, although nearer to Tan-y-bwlch conditions became much worse. Light-coloured patterns on the wall reveal missing tiles from the roof. The lamp bracket has been moved since the earlier pictures were taken.
J. S. Griffiths

Below:
Conway Castle, unfinished and in primer, at Minffordd on 9 March 1986. The roof of the station house has subsequently lost its shaped slates. *Author*

Minffordd Yard

Top:
Minffordd Yard was opened in 1872, jointly developed by the Cambrian Railways and the FR. It was a Spooner creation, designed primarily to facilitate the transfer of slate from narrow to standard gauge and coal in the reverse direction, having tracks on different levels for this purpose. Different parts of the yard were leased to different companies; in this pre-1922 picture to: Davies & Sons (the last area to remain in slate company use, until the 1970s) on the left; Maenofferen, both slate sheds; North Wales Slate Co, to the left of the two-storey flour store. The slate sheds have had their roofs raised and are now used to store rolling stock. The standard gauge Minffordd station is to the right of this picture. *Author's Collection*

Above:
A train of loaded slate wagons, which have been brought down by gravity from Blaenau Ffestiniog, standing on the line into the yard from the FR main line. Behind the third wagon three men have posed for the camera. This area was leased to the Oakeley Quarry and that behind the standard gauge wagons to Votty & Bowydd. Legible branding on the standard gauge wagons identify those belonging to the Great Western Railway, London & South Western Railway and the Midland Railway. *Author's Collection*

Top:
The low level sidings were originally for importing coal, using the chutes on the right. Now that the standard gauge sidings have gone, removed in the 1970s, the sidings are used to receive ballast brought in by road. The storage of oil at this location allows it to be decanted without using pumps. Wagon No 66 has a Boston Lodge-built underframe and bogies imported from Poland in 1973; the tank has a capacity for 2,000gall. The locomotive is *Moel Hebog. FR Co*

Above:
The Goods Shed is now the permanent way store and the Civil Engineering Department's rolling stock is kept within it. Wagon No 62, being shunted by *Prince* on 20 October 1991, also has Polish bogies; the underframe has been adapted from a road trailer. The tank capacity is 1,800gall. *Author*

From 19th to 20th Century

During the later years of the 19th century the Festiniog Railway reached its peak, culminating in the construction, in 1879 and 1886, of two double engines, *Merddin Emrys* and *Livingston Thompson*, in its own Boston Lodge Works. The first was designed by George Percival Spooner, whose father, Charles Easton Spooner, had an imaginative streak which had helped bring the railway to public attention. In turn, it had been Charles Easton Spooner's father, James Spooner, who had participated in surveying the railway's route before construction began. It is no coincidence that the era of the Festiniog Railway's pre-eminence in the field of narrow-gauge railways coincided with the period in which the Spooners were involved with the Railway.

Charles Easton Spooner died in November 1889. During his career with the railway he had been, variously, Company Secretary, Treasurer and Locomotive Superintendent. This brief list does not give a true impression of his impact on the FR. John Sylvester Hughes, Company Secretary since 1887, became General Manager and Engineer in October 1889. On 3 February 1890 he submitted this report to the Board:

Merddin Emrys
Below:
The construction of *Merddin Emrys* was authorised in 1877, having first been considered the previous year. It was thought that £450 could be saved by building the locomotive at Boston Lodge, although it is not clear if this amount included the construction of the erecting shop authorised to 'accommodate the work'. The design was again by G. P. Spooner and produced a larger locomotive than *James Spooner*. Photographed in front of the Britannia Foundry on 19 September 1895, at 12.30pm, a new boiler was fitted the following year.
Hayley Gordon Brierley/Kirklees Cultural Services Collection

Festiniog Railway
Engineer & General Manager's Report
To the Directors
Gentlemen

I have the honour to inform you that I took over the whole charge of the Line on the 1st October last and gave notice in the usual way to all those connected or having dealings with us.

In the following month it was my sad duty to inform you of the death of my predecessor who had been for so many years connected with the Railway.

I examined and went through all the papers and plans of the Railway.

I made a careful inspection of the whole of the Buildings, Works, Bridges, Culverts, Breastwalls, Fencing and Permanent Way and Signals also the Machinery and Rolling Stock and made notes respecting same for present and future guidance.

I got the Wagons carefully counted so as to be satisfied that the number in the accounts were really existent and the results were satisfactory.

A length of 904 yards of Permanent Way was laid = 40½ tons making a total length of 15,096 yards laid with steel rails, leaving 4,008 yards or 2½ miles of Main Line still to complete. When prices of iron seemed likely to go up considerably I communicated with the Chairman as to buying 100 tons which was done giving a saving on present quotation of £220.

There is at present in stock 160 tons and it will require another 180 tons to complete the laying of the Main Line with Steel Rails. It is a question whether it would not be advisable to buy these now. The price which will be got for the old rails will probably go far towards meeting the cost if they are kept for some time.

Relaying will commence as soon as the days lengthen and the weather gets settled.

Enquiry was sent out for prices for 12 months contract for materials which have not yet been accepted. The contract for coal is now to be accepted, prices for which I place before you.

Big Quay The works at the Big Quay (Cei Mawr) were completed during the Halfyear the total cost being £1,079 2 4 (£1,079.12). In addition to this the Land owner wanted £20 0 0 compensation and the stone Quarry fenced in and afterwards kept in repair and the Tenant £3 0 0. I have been able to get this settled at £12 12 0 (£12.60) and £2 respectively, and the Quarry to be fenced

with wire fencing but not kept in repair afterwards. This makes with £3 3 0 (£3.15) Law Expenses the total amount £1096 17 4 (£1096.87) plus cost of fencing say £10, £1106 17 4 (£1106.87).

The suspense account stands at £284 9 2 (£284.46) to which has to be added the above amounts £27 15 0 (£27.75) which will be paid off in 3 Halfyears in accordance with the resolution passed.

The new carriage sheds at Boston Lodge have been completed the total cost being £202 0 10 (£202.04).

Locomotives The Locomotive *James Spooner* was completed during the Halfyear and is equal to new the total cost was £769 15 0 (£769.75). The original cost of this Engine was £2,135 10 0 (£2,135.50).

There are now out of the nine Locomotives, 3 Double Bogie Engines in thorough order and also 1 single Boiler and 2 four wheel Engines. The other three engines are from 22 to 25 years of age and it is impossible to say when they may break down. If the tubes gave way they would not be worth repairing and it would be necessary to make them up the same as the others with new Boilers and Frames. The gearing is good and there are plates in stock for the tanks of the *Welsh Pony* and also a set of Tyres for the Wheels. It is advisable that a decision be now made in regard to reconstruction of this Engine. The Frameplate of the *Giant* which engine was made up in 1888, but the frames were not then renewed is found to be cracked and will require a new one the cost of which will be about £10. The cost of remaking the Pony would be about £420.

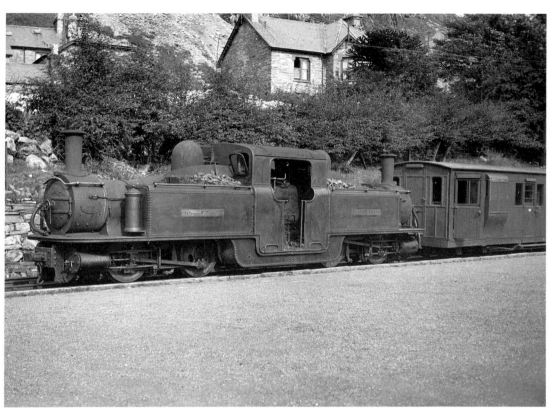

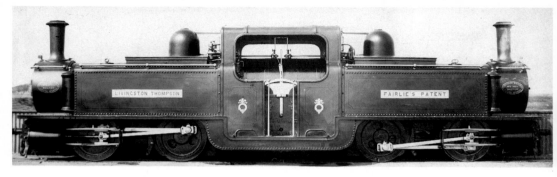

Coal trucks It was passed at the Board meeting February 1889 that 10 new coal Wagons should be made the cost of which would have been £35 each. There has lately been complaints of the want of these. I found that we had 20 lowsided and stone trucks which would carry about ½ ton of coal and as they were not required have had 16 altered at a cost each of £1 12 6 (£1.62) to carry 1 ton to 1½ tons each. The cost of a new Truck being £18. There are also 24 Slab trucks of which but few are now required and these I am now altering into iron coal trucks to carry 2 to 2½ tons by putting iron sides on at a cost of £9 10 0 (£9.50) each as against £35 for new Wagons. There are at present 6 in hand and the number will be further increased as required.

One new Quarrymen's carriage was completed and 2 Wagons for carrying Pigs & Calves have been made from 2 of the old Workmens carriages.

Land The purchase of a piece of land at Penrhyn which had been negotiated for many years ago was completed and the money paid amounting to £117 0 2 (£117.01) and been charged to Capital.

Telegraph The Oakeley Slate Company and Messrs Greaves having decided to have a private telegraph between the Quarries and Wharves, negotiations were entered into with Messrs Saunders & Co for erection and for Way Leave over our Line. This was agreed to at a charge of 7s/6d (37.5p) per wire per mile per annum for Way Leave until the termination of Messrs Saunders' contract for the maintenance of our wires which takes place on the 12th March 1892. They completed the work beginning of January. I took the opportunity of looking

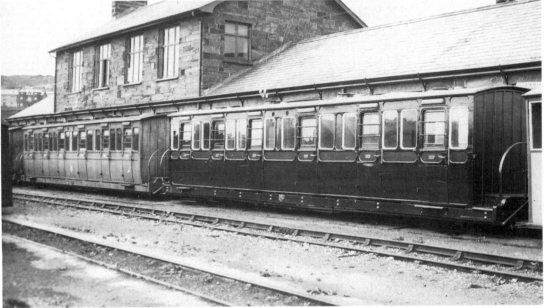

Livingston Thompson

Top left:

It was in 1882 that construction of a further double engine, to replace *Little Wonder*, was authorised. Using the same basic design as for *Merddin Emrys*, but with modifications by William Williams, the Works manager, the result was *Livingston Thompson*, which was completed in 1885. The photograph was taken on the Cob in 1887; the fence behind was painted white, the better to show off the rolling stock posed before it — photographs of the Harbour and Station taken several years later showed the white fence still. *R. H. Bleasdale*

Above left:

In 1939 *Livingston Thompson/Taliesin* went into Boston Lodge for repairs which remained uncompleted when the railway closed in 1946. Consequently the locomotive was in comparatively good order in 1955 and was quite easily restored the following year. It is shown at Harbour station, still in undercoat, during trials in the autumn of 1956. *A. F. Porter*

19th CENTURY BOGIE STOCK

Top:

Car No 20, one of two built by the Gloucester Wagon Co in 1879, was brought out as an example of the very latest in FR passenger rolling stock when photographed in 1887. It came back into service in 1957 and given a major body repair 30 years later. *R. H. Bleasdale*

Above:

Nos 17 and 18 were, in 1876, the last vehicles built for the FR by Brown, Marshalls & Co. They have wrought iron frames but not the integral wrought iron body framing of Nos 15 and 16. When Nos 17 and 18 were photographed at Harbour station between the wars No 18 was obviously not long out of the paint shop. The curve in the bodyside of Nos 17-20 is the reason for them being called 'bow-siders' on the railway. *R. E. Tustin Collection*

into Messrs Saunders' contract for maintenance and asked them to supply me with particulars which they did but it did not agree with mine. They also sent in an account for £12 12 0 (£12.60) extra charge which they made out was due to Sept 30th last. I sent them a statement showing that they had overcharged £49 10 0 (£49.50) making a difference of £62 2 0 (62.10) between the two accounts which by end of Agreement would have amounted to £84 3 3 (£84.16).

The telegraph line is now in very good order most of the poles having been renewed. It will most likely be found that it will not be advisable to renew the

maintenance contract at the end of the present Agreement, and that it can be done at much less cost.

Insurance I named at the last Board Meeting that it appeared to me that the rate paid for Insurance to the Royal Insurance Company was high and there were many new buildings not included. I communicated with the Insurance Co and asked them to give a new rate, and also with the Alliance Company — the result was that the latter was accepted — the amount insured being for the Stations & Buildings £5,910 and Boston Lodge Buildings & Rolling Stock £6,355 a total of £12,265 at an annual premium of £20 2 9

Left:
Car No 17's second body overhaul since revival was completed in 1990, when a great deal of attention had been given to replacing items which had been removed, such as mouldings and ventilator hoods, to ease maintenance in the 1960s. Whilst apparently attending only to the vehicle's vintage appearance, modern materials have been used where they give the best result; the ply panels for the sides are faced in aluminium! The finished vehicle was photographed on 20 October 1991. *Author*

Below left:
Nos 21 and 22, was built for the tourist traffic by the Ashbury Carriage & Wagon Co in 1886; this firm had previously built similar stock for the North Wales Narrow Gauge Railways. No 22 was back in service in 1958 but No 21 was dismantled in 1962, being considered too decrepit to be worthy of restoration. No 23, one of the NWNGR cars, became one of the two carriages used in 1955. Another such vehicle, No 26, was obtained in 1959, having been a hen house at Groeslon since 1942. No 22 received a steel underframe in 1967 and a new body in 1984. The NWNGR cars had half doors when built and were first restored thus; full doors replaced these in 1965/66. No 22 was photographed on 20 October 1991. *Author*

Below:
For the Society's 1956 AGM, held on 24 March, the two carriages then in service, Nos 12 and 23, were assembled at Portmadoc with three unrestored cars and the then unrestored *Merddin Emrys*. *FR Co*

(£20.14) as against £9,330 and £25 15 9 (£25.79) respectively under the old policy shewing a gain of £2,935 in the amount insured at a less cost of £5 13 0 (£5.65) per annum.

Railway Rates In regard to the Railway Rates Act 1888 the committee appointed to take evidence &c has not yet finished the enquiry. I have supplied all the information required and was glad to be able to state that there was no opposition from Local freighters, in which respect I think we stand unique.

Railway Regulation The Board of Trade under the Powers granted by the Railway Regulation Act 1889 gave notice that the following must be carried out.

1st All tickets to have the fares stamped on them by the (1 July 1890)

2nd The Block System to be carried out by (within 12 months)

3rd The interlocking of all points and Signals to be carried out in (within 18 months)

4th Continuous Automatic Brakes to be carried out in (within 18 months)

As they agreed to answer any suggestion made by my Company respective to above requirements I prepared a Memorial which was approved by the Board and I forwarded it to the Board of Trade and at the same time named that the Directors would be glad to meet the Authorities if required.

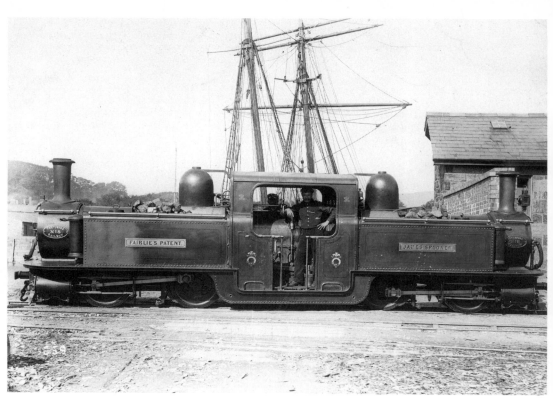

James Spooner

Left:
Built in 1872 by the Avonside Engine Co of Bristol, *James Spooner* was designed by George Percival Spooner. It is shown at the Harbour at the turn of the century. *Loco Pub Co*

Below left:
James Spooner, looking rather worn, is pictured outside the old locomotive shed at Boston Lodge, probably in the 1920s. The locomotive had been fitted with new frames in 1919 but required a new boiler in 1926. The boiler was not replaced but the locomotive was used again from 1928 to 1930, failing regularly, before being finally withdrawn. *Author's Collection*

I found that representatives of single line Railways had met and discussed the above requirements and their views were sent to the Railway Association who communicated with the authorities.

From these it appears the Board of Trade will deal with each Company on its own merits.

The last communication received in answer to the Memorial requires statements to be filled up on the form given and which I now lay before you for approval.

Messrs Saunders sent in prices for completing the Block System and I got prices also from other parties. There does not seem so far to be much competition in this class of work as there is in Signalling and Brakes but no doubt there will be from this on.

I have also received an answer to my application with particulars and various prices from makers of Signals and Brakes. All these can be held over until a decision is given by the Board of Trade.

A Bill has been deposited this Session entitled the Beddgelert & Rhyddu Railway which forms a connecting line between the Croesor Railway and the North Wales Narrow Gauge Railway via Beddgelert. A Bill has also been deposited for extension of time for completing the NWN Gauge Rly from Dinas to Carnarvon on the 1ft 11½in gauge. If these were carried out it would form a continuous narrow gauge from Blaenau Festiniog to Carnarvon.

Traffic The Summer traffic was not very satisfactory the weather having been wet until late in the season. The new circular route from Barmouth and other places on the coast via the Cambrian, Festiniog, and Great Western was opened last Summer, our proportion from the Great Western was

£7 8 2 (£7.41) as against £2 4 0 (£2.20) in the corresponding half. The receipts from the Circular Tours by Rail and Coach in connection with the L&NW Rly having resulted in £135 0 9 (£135.04) against £112 19 5 (£112.97)) the previous season. I have been in communication with the Cambrian and L&NW Rlys in regard to further extending the arrangement of cheap through tickets to various places.

The Goods Traffic in connection with the Steamship Rebecca for Blaenau Festiniog and different places between Portmadoc and Blaenau is increasing being £33 11 7 (£33.57½) as against £21 4 3 (£21.21½) the corresponding half.

The Coal traffic from Vessels for the Quarries is keeping up favourably and also the Through Goods traffic arrangement with the Great Western Railway. The quantity of Slates sent inland by rail from Blaenau by the L&NW Rly was 5,671 tons as against 5,187 tons, by Great Western 9,178 tons as against 7,497 tons; and from Minffordd by the Cambrian 17,503 tons as compared with 17,065 tons in the corresponding half and by Vessels from Portmadoc 58,158 tons as against 54,785 tons in the corresponding half.

The Slate traffic to Portmadoc has unfortunately fallen off throughout the Half year consequent on less make at the quarries the demand being slack for the Home Market.

Royal Visit During the Half year the Princess Beatrice and Prince Henry went up the Line as far as Plâs Tanybwlch from Minffordd and everything passed off most successfully and they expressed themselves highly interested with the trip.

On completion of the Big Quay and the carriage sheds the Masons and Labourers who had been employed were discharged. By the end of the year I got all other repairs done on the Line and discharged the 3 regular hands who had always been kept on viz Mason, Rockman and Labourer. The number of hands at Boston Lodge were also reduced by 3. This has been made possible by the new system of trains running for the winter.

The one extra hand which appears under the Head of Permanent Way is Hugh Williams the oldest workman on the Line. It had become too risky for him to act as a platelayer, and he is now kept on for weeding and helping with the repairs of the fencing and odd jobs.

The one extra under the head of Traffic is the clerk in the Secretary's Office who was not included before.

There has been a rise of Wages on the adjoining Railways and in the District and some additions have also had to be made to some of our men to keep them from leaving.

Half yearly Accounts On reference to account No 12 Abstract A it will be seen that there is an increase under the head of Permanent Way of £147 15 9 (£147.78½) which arises from the extra cost of relaying with Steel Rails. Under the head of repairs of Roads, Bridges, Signals, Station Buildings there is an extra cost of £76 18 4 (£76.92). This is accounted for by the Masons and men being put on for repairs for 3 months remaining of the year as they had been engaged altogether on the Big Quay for 2 years, and the supply of new platform lamps for the stations instead of those worn out. The oil for the latter will be only about half the price of that formerly used.

Abstract B — The increase of £39 11 3 (£39.56½) is due to the increased prices of stores — in other respects there is a decrease.

Abstract C — The increase of £132 7 0 (£132.35) is more than accounted for by the new carriage shed of £202 0 10 (£202.04).

Abstract D — There is a reduction of £56 7 2 (£56.36).

Abstract E — The increase in special expenditure was caused by the Royal Visit amounting to £30 but there is a decrease in the total of £45 9 6 (£45.47½).

The Permanent Way Stores on hand amounted to £1,030 10 11 (£1,030.59½) as compared with £700 19 4 (£700.97) in the corresponding half and the loco and other stores £1,986 6 6 (£1,986.32½) as compared with £2,001 13 3 (£2,001.66½).

The amount carried over to next Halfyear for the purpose of comparing with the corresponding Halfyear should be £540 1 2 (£540.06) but as the Auditors decided that in account No 11 the Income Tax should not be deducted this appears as £509 8 8 (£509.44). The credit for Income Tax will appear in the current Halfyear's Accounts.

By comparison with the corresponding Half year it will be seen that the amount carried forward from the present Halfyear was £155 17 5 (£155.87) as against £402 16 9 (£402.83½) difference of £246 19 4 (£246.96½) and if to this is added £202 0 10 (£202.04) for New Carriage Shed

= £449 0 2 (£449.01) out of which has to be deducted the difference between £540 1 2 (£540.06) and £658 5 7 (£658.28) = £118 4 5 (£118.22) leaving £330 15 9 (£330.78½) which nearly meets the 1% difference in the Dividend.

A large descriptive Timetable placard with the map of the Line and connections with it would be advisable for putting up at the Railway Stations along the Coast and elsewhere for the summer.

I am Gentlemen
Your Obedient Servant
J. S. Hughes

Whilst Hughes proved not to have the Spooner touch, this report does show his commitment to containing costs, surely something with which any board would be pleased. The £202 carriage shed was the structure which was damaged by rock falls during the closure; the site is now that of the locomotive shed. The report does show how history repeats itself; work on Cei Mawr, repairing the culvert, was being undertaken as this text was being completed in the autumn of 1991. Hughes's desire to attract tourists should not go unnoticed — he could not have foreseen that 100 years later tourists would provide the railway's only source of traffic. It is interesting, too, to note that a Royal visit could be accommodated for £30! It took place on 27 August 1889, when Charles Easton Spooner presented an

Taliesin
Right:
Also designed by G. P. Spooner, *Taliesin* was built at the Vulcan Foundry in 1876. The front end of the locomotive was dimensionally identical to *James Spooner;* the back end, as built, had much in common with the single Fairlies built by the same firm for the North Wales Narrow Gauge Railways. By the time this photograph was taken the rear bogie had been replaced, the bunker enlarged, the cab profile reduced, plates placed over the lower rear windows to prevent damage whilst coaling, a grab handle fixed to the smokebox and the makers' sand pots replaced by the Festiniog standard model. *Loco Pub Co*

Right:
In 1899/1900 *Taliesin* received an overhaul which included the fitting of a new boiler and cylinders and an overall cab. It is shown arriving at Tan-y-bwlch in the early years of the century. One of the two 1880-built bogie vans is coupled next to the engine. The 1990s *Taliesin* replica will not look unlike the locomotive shown here, except that for size it will have more in common with *Merddin Emrys* than *James Spooner.* In the foreground are the slate empties attached to an Up passenger train. *Author's Collection*

album of local photographs to the Princess. Hughes resigned as General Manager on 31 December 1908.

With the arrival of the 20th century the FR was to enter a period of decline which was to end, in 1946, in closure and abandonment. The decline was caused both by the tapping of the Blaenau slate traffic by the LNWR (from 1881) and the GWR (from 1883) and the development of alternative roofing materials. In practical terms the real decline stemmed from a labour dispute which closed the quarries in 1913. Reduced income prevented the railway from meeting its maintenance commitments and it was never to overcome the arrears, as the Railway came under Government control following the outbreak of war in 1914. Part of Boston Lodge Works was commandeered for the manufacture of shells — the first time that women were allowed to work there. The Locomotive Superintendent, Robert Williams, was put in charge of the shell factory but in 1915 he still found time to complete his report for the FR Company directors on the condition of locomotives and rolling stock for the half year ending 30 June 1915:

I have carefully inspected as far as possible the Loco Engines, and Rolling Stock, and beg to report on same as follows:-

Locomotive Engines
Double
Merddin Emrys — In working condition. Requires heavy repairs new tyres, Tubes &c. Working pressure 140lbs. Age of boiler 18½ Years.
James Spooner — In good working condition. Working pressure 170lbs. Age of boiler 7½ Years.
Livingston Thompson — In good working condition. The Tanks as previously reported are in a very thin condition. Working pressure 160lbs. Age of boiler 10 Years.
Single
Little Giant — In working condition. Boiler requires a patch. Working pressure 160lbs. Age of boiler 10½ Years.
Welsh Pony — Rebuilt and completed all but painting, been out for trial and working satisfactory. Working Pressure 160lbs.
Princess — In working condition. Working pressure 140lbs. Age of boiler 20 Years.
Prince — Now taken in. Boiler & Tyres worn out, having been running for 22 years & 11

months making a total mileage approximately for the period of 407,161 Miles (This gives a yearly average of 17,700, yet according to Spring, paragraph 158, later, in 1913 the total annual mileage for shunting and pilotage was only 13,366. 107,161 is probably the correct figure — PJ)
Palmerston — In good working condition. Working pressure 160lbs. Age of boiler 5 Years.
Taliesin — In working condition. Boiler requires patching, and thorough overhauling, also new Tubes. Working pressure 150lbs. Age of boiler 15½ Years.
Five Tenders — Four in order, and one under Repairs.
Rolling Stock
Carriages & Vans — All in good running condition, One Third class carriage at Works to be rebuilt. Also Bogie Carriage No 18 requires Sett (sic) Cast Steel Wheels. One First Class compartment in Bogie Carriages No 17 & 18 to be upholstered anew. Materials on hand, also Sett of cast Steel Wheels on hand for Bogie Carriage No 16. The woodwork of two Vans previously reported not yet renewed.
Quarrymen's Carriages — In working condition. 8 at Works to be rebuilt, also the wheels on some of these carriages are worn very thin, and new ones must be replaced.
Iron Coal Trucks — In good working condition. Some at Works for ordinary repairs.
Iron Slate Wagons — In good working condition. Several at Works for ordinary repairs.
Wooden Slate Wagons — In good working condition. Some at Works for ordinary repairs.
Timber Trucks — In fair working condition. 9½ pairs now at Works in need of repairs and renewals.
Stone Trucks — In fair working condition, excepting those that are now at Works to be repaired and renewed.
Coal & Goods Trucks — In fair working condition, 10 at Works to be rebuilt, and some for ordinary repairs.
Robert Williams
Loco Supt.
July 16th 1915

Penrhyn

Below:
Penrhyn station was opened in 1865 and photographed here in 1887. The main structure dates from 1879, using materials from the original Harbour station building. It lies above the village of Penrhyndeudraeth, location of a standard gauge station, in the area known as Pen-y-bwlch.
R. H. Bleasdale

Below centre:
Some three miles from Portmadoc, Penrhyn was re-opened in 1957, when a run-round loop was installed. The site between the goods shed and the station had been occupied by a Co-op store; when this was vacated in the 1960s it was decided to modify the station to accommodate volunteers. Bedrooms were installed in the station building, a kitchen and living/dining room in the Co-op building; and a new ablutions block (with the flat roof, in the November 1981 photograph) linked the two. The loop was removed after the introduction of Rhiw Goch as a passing place in 1975. *Author*

Bottom:
At the end of the 1980s work commenced on restoring Penrhyn to the appearance it had in the Bleasdale photograph. A considerable amount of effort had been put in when the project was approaching completion and photographed on 26 October 1991. The platform has been modified to comply with modern safety requirements but the signboard, chimney stacks and barge-boards were all installed to match the photograph. Not visible in this photograph is the wagon turntable which has been re-installed outside the goods shed (and not noticeable is the false pitched roof installed above the ablutions block). It is not unlikely that the McKenzie & Holland signal post will make a reappearance, too. Internally the building has been rewired, re-plumbed and insulated, to give the best possible standard of accommodation for the railway's volunteers. *Author*

FESTINIOG RAILWAY.
QUARRYMAN'S DAILY TICKET 6d.
Available in Quarrymen's Carriage only
NOT TRANSFERABLE
PENRHYN
TO
DDUALLT
Note—Issued subject to the conditions and regulations in the Company's Time Tables Books Bills and Notices and to the special conditions named on other side

2186

Tan-y-bwlch

Above left:
Tan-y-bwlch, the largest of the FR's intermediate stations, is seven miles from Portmadoc and was opened in 1873, mainly serving the Plas Tan-y-bwlch estate. All Up steam trains take water here. The barn structure was intended as a passenger shelter but was replaced by a cottage c1896. The footbridge, demolished in 1933, marks a right-of-way through the station. The centre road crosses the up loop line to serve the goods shed and coal drops. There are two wagons visible behind the footbridge steps in this 1887 view. *R. H. Bleasdale*

Left:
James Spooner pulls into Tan-y-bwlch c1910. The cottage is being extended, the centre road has been removed and a horse watches proceedings over the fence. *Commercial postcard — Kingsway Series*

Below left:
At Tan-y-bwlch the railway runs around Llyn Mair, an artificial lake built for landscaping purposes. Following re-opening in 1958 the goods shed was adapted as a café, shop and booking office; toilets were provided in timber buildings, replacing, for men, the open-air urinal behind the water tower. The train, photographed on 1 September 1972, consists of: *Alistair*, a 13hp Ruston which once rescued a passenger train; a slate wagon with one end removed; and van No 59, built by the Great Western Railway for the Vale of Rheidol section in 1923. *John Scrace*

Right:
Tan-y-bwlch was the terminus until 1968, during which period the layout was modified to create an island platform and a new footbridge was installed. On 26 October 1991 *Conway Castle* arrives with a Down train, to pass *Prince* with a terminating special of vintage stock — from the loco, 1865 'Bug Box' No 5, 1872 No 16, 1880 No 12, 1875 hearse van and 1885 van No 2. *Author*

Between the Wars

After the War the FR found itself, in 1921, released from public control and with a new board of directors with limited (if any) railway operating experience. The new directors were Henry Joseph Jack, Evan R. Davies and Sir John H. Stewart, who were also involved with the Aluminium Corporation Ltd at Dolgarrog and who were to become directors of the North Wales Narrow Gauge Railways Co in 1922. Additionally Jack had also had an interest in the Portmadoc, Beddgelert & South Snowdon Railway since 1919 and Davies, a solicitor, had gone to London, from Pwllheli, to set up a legal practice there with David Lloyd George. The Snowdon Mountain Railway also came into the same sphere of influence and Davies's descendants are still associated with it.

Jack was interested in using his interests in the Portmadoc, Beddgelert & South Snowdon and the North Wales Narrow Gauge Railways to complete the much talked-about link of the latter with the Croesor Tramway and Portmadoc, via Beddgelert — what was to become the Welsh Highland Railway. Electrification was the ultimate aim, to the benefit of the associated North Wales Power & Traction Co Ltd. Major G. C. Spring, a consultant, was asked to give his opinion on the state of the railways and their operation. He did so as follows:

(All capitalisation and emphasis are as the original; some punctuation has been added. Spelling has also been corrected - the Major had particular problems with the Welsh place names and 'personnel' was always rendered 'personal'. The sections on the Croesor Tramway and the NWNGR have been excluded, as have a number of clauses of a more general nature. On the subject of the NWNGR, Spring considered that a passenger service which would pay its way could be readily restored between Dinas and South Snowdon, but that the service would be more worthwhile and more profitable if the narrow-gauge line were extended alongside the standard gauge to Caernarvon, to avoid the break of gauge.)

REPORT FROM G. C. SPRING
THE FESTINIOG RAILWAY
I GENERAL
1 In order to deduce the potentialities of a business, a description of the existing conditions of such business is necessary.
2 The Railway was originally constructed as a horse drawn tramway to transport slates from the Quarries of Blaenau Festiniog to the seaport of Portmadoc, a distance of approximately 13½ miles.

This was converted in 1869 to a steam railroad adapted to the conveyance of passengers.
3 The isolated position rendered necessary facilities for rolling stock construction and repairs, with which it is now equipped on a larger scale than are other feeder lines, where such are generally provided by the mother railway.
4 In 1879, transhipment junctions were constructed at Blaenau Festiniog with the L&NWR, and a few years later with the GWR.
5 The valley of the Glaslyn river traversed by the railway is sparsely populated, generally speaking by persons dependent on the quarrying industry at Festiniog. *(The Major appears to have overlooked the fact that for most of its length the Railway runs through the valley of the Dwyryd.)*
7 The railway carries the following traffic:
    a Mineral (slate &c) and goods.
    b Local passengers including quarry workmen.
    c Summer season passenger tourist traffic.
8 The goods and mineral tonnage for 1920 (78,829 tons) provided 54% of the gross receipts. The principal items of this are given below:

Slates	52,294 tons
Granite & stone setts	15,786 tons
Coal	3,337 tons
Iron & Steel materials	230 tons
Flour and grain	672 tons
Building sand	230 tons

slates being the largest and most important.
9 Owing to the regular and constant falling grade of the line (ruling 1 in 66) it is possible to run trains consisting of from 50 to 120 full slate wagons ... weighing on an average 3 tons each from the mineral or marshalling siding at Glan-y-pwll Box to Minffordd Junction without the aid of engine power, under the control of brake fitted slate wagons in the proportion of 1 in 5.

Two brakesmen normally work this train down unless the rails are exceedingly greasy when a porter is taken from Duffws to assist.

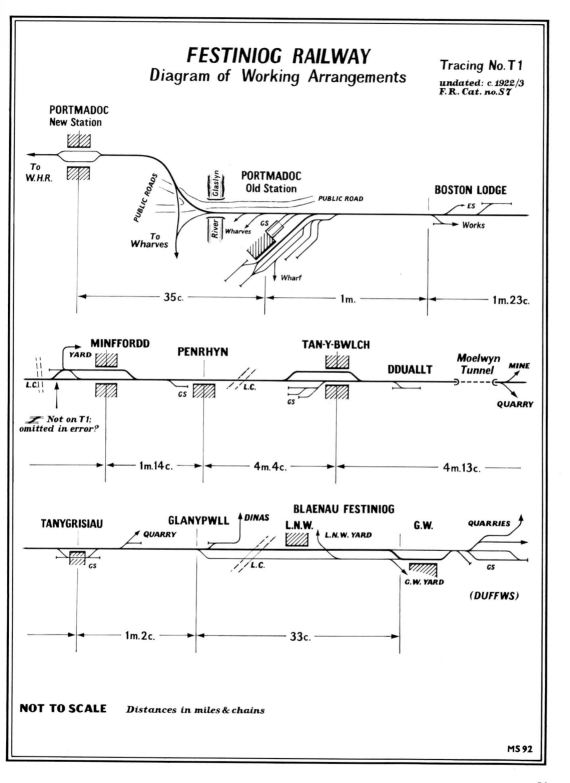

FESTINIOG RAILWAY
Diagram of Working Arrangements

Tracing No. T1

undated: c.1922/3
F.R. Cat. no. S7

PORTMADOC
New Station

To
W.H.R.

PUBLIC ROADS

To
Wharves

Glaslyn

River

Wharves

GS

PORTMADOC
Old Station

PUBLIC ROAD

Wharf

BOSTON LODGE

ES

Works

|← 35c. →|← 1m. →|← 1m.23c. →|

MINFFORDD

YARD

PENRHYN

GS

L.C.

TAN-Y-BWLCH

GS

DDUALLT

**Moelwyn
Tunnel**

MINE

QUARRY

L.C.

*Not on T1;
omitted in error?*

|← 1m.14c. →|← 4m.4c. →|← 4m.13c. →|

TANYGRISIAU

GS

GLANYPWLL

QUARRY

DINAS

BLAENAU FESTINIOG

L.N.W.

L.N.W. YARD

G.W.

G.W. YARD

QUARRIES

GS

L.C.

(DUFFWS)

|← 1m.2c. →|← 33c. →|

NOT TO SCALE   *Distances in miles & chains*

MS 92

10 From Minffordd Junction engine power is required to haul along the flat into Portmadoc station and wharves, and to place wagons into owners' sidings at Minffordd Jct for stacking and transhipment of slates to the Cambrian Railway.

11 Two slate trains are run down from the mineral lines at Duffws and Glan-y-pwll, and empty wagons are attached to the rear of the up passenger trains for return.

The shunting engine at the Duffws end of the line (see par 17), in cases where head winds prevail, pushes this slate train over a flat gradient until on the 1 in 66.

It does not appear possible to attach these slate trains to the back of the passenger trains since the addition of from 250 to 300 tons would exceed the braking power of the passenger train, and would therefore entail brakesmen on the mineral portion, so that there would be no monetary saving. Also the Board of Trade do not advise the running of mixed trains with more than 25 wagons attached, which number would be exceeded twofold or more.

It would moreover be most difficult unless a very low rate of speed were maintained to draw up trains at station platforms.

12 It is noted that two brakesmen leave Portmadoc by the workmen's train at 5.30am in order to brake the 9.55am slate train down from Duffws, and are booked off at Minffordd Duffws at 3.20pm and 4.15pm respectively, thus both incurring overtime. It is suggested that payment of overtime could be obviated.

13 At the Moelwyn Halt there are two sidings controlled by a key attached to the train staff of the section, the Moelwyn Mine

Moelwyn

Below:
A second World War 1 locomotive, built by Baldwin in the USA in 1918, was obtained in 1925. Apparently not as useful as the Simplex it reportedly spent much time out of use, indeed this photograph being taken outside the Boston Lodge loco shed, on 8 July 1936, suggests that it was pulled out for the photographer. However, it was brought into service in 1956 and named *Moelwyn*. In 1957 a leading pony truck was added to improve the ride. The locomotive has seen very little use in recent years and is ready to become a museum piece when the Railway has a museum large enough to house it. Restoration to working order is to commence in 1992. *S. W. Baker*

and Brooke's quarry. The former is at present not working, whilst the output of the latter is cleared in trains of not less than fifteen wagons, when offered, by the shunting engine situated at Duffws, and placed in the L&NWR tranship sidings at Blaenau Festiniog.

14 The roadside local goods business is small, loaded coal wagons being detached from up mixed trains and hand shunted into sidings.

SHUNTING

15 Two shunting engines are constantly in steam, viz:
    1 At Minffordd Junction and Portmadoc
    2 At Duffws and Dinas Branch.

The shunting mileage is very large being about 17% of the loaded train mileage for 1920.

16 No 1 sorts and distributes slate loaded wagons into the various owners' wharves, marshals and forms empty wagons for return to Duffws and also draws occasional loaded slate wagons from the stacking wharves at Portmadoc to the yard at Minffordd.

17 No 2 is during the summer season stabled at Dinas Engine Shed but during the slack season at Boston Lodge. During such latter months this engine travels up light or draws any loads that may accrue from roadside stations, such as Moelwyn (Brookes Quarry Siding) and spends the remainder of the day in clearing and marshalling the slate wagons to and from the various slate quarries, the inclines of which are at varying distances from Duffws terminus.

18 There are thus daily two Engines in steam whose Engine mileage is mostly non-productive but whose cost must be borne. The shunting required on other Railway quarry line systems by the necessity of marshalling the various owners' wagons into train or station order is entirely absent since all slate wagons are the Company's property and can be used indiscriminately for any quarry.

19 The average number of wagons dealt with at Portmadoc and Minffordd Jct daily is 50 and 100 respectively.

20 The shunting of wagons at intermediate stations for roadside goods purposes is generally carried out by hand.

PASSENGER TRAFFIC

21 The Glaslyn valley is sparsely populated and such as exists is mainly dependent on the quarries at Festiniog for a living.

The average number of workmen carried daily during the first six months of 1921 was 220 per day. The average number of passengers carried throughout the months of May to August inclusive were 9,000 per month and during the remaining 8 months 7,600 per month irrespective of workmen in both cases.

The total number of passengers carried during 1920 was 117,843.

II TIME TABLE

The Time Table as at present arranged, ie for the Summer months, provides for a workmen's train up and down, the seven passenger trains up and eight down, between the hours of 8.20am and 10.7pm. An up Goods train leaves Portmadoc at 6.35am and arrives at Duffws at 7.42am, two down unengined slate trains leave Duffws at 9.55 and 12.55 respectively and the Portmadoc Shunting Engine hauls slate and goods wagons between Portmadoc and Minffordd and vice versa twice daily.

24 Empty slate wagons when released at Portmadoc or Minffordd are attached to all upgoing passenger trains in such numbers as the haulage power of the engine will permit.

25 Since these wagons are not fitted with Vacuum brakes they are controlled by the brakesmen (on their return journey up to Duffws) who brought them down.

26 The Winter time table provides for the up and down Workmen's train and 4 up and down passenger trains and 2 slate trains.

27 A passenger train leaving Portmadoc at 9pm and reaching Duffws at 10 pm and a train leaving Duffws at 9.10pm and reaching Portmadoc at 10.7pm has been recently put on.

28 Whilst it is axiomatic that a train newly added to a timetable requires the best of at least a year's running before its paying capacity can be gauged, and whilst it is incorrect to assume that a late train merely detracts from the load of earlier trains, since the fact of there being such late trains is generally the reason for a journey being taken, two important points arise.

    1 Late trains involve overtime rates for all running staff.

    2 It is necessary to send 2 engines and 2 crews to Duffws by the train arriving at 7.20pm, one engine standing under steam with an idle crew until 9.10pm, nearly 2 hours, since the last down train is unbalanced.

Goods stock

Above:
The FR had little non-slate goods traffic. It included some coal for Tan-y-bwlch and Blaenau Ffestiniog, materials for the quarries and flour for the (still extant) bakery near Penrhyn Station. The photograph, taken on 14 April 1946, shows two covered wagons used for the flour traffic at Penrhyn. The six-wheeled wagon, built 1880, has a Cleminson's Patent flexible wheelbase and was built to carry coal, with a capacity of six tons. Having doors at one end only, its roof was added when the vehicle carried cattle in connection with an agricultural show in Portmadoc. Until October 1991 the wagon was displayed, without roof or floor, outside the Harbour Station museum. The four-wheeled van, No 101, probably dates from around 1875 and also has doors at one end only. *R. E. Tustin*

Left:
One of the covered four-wheel vans (now No 154) survives and is used as a mobile tool store by the Civil Engineering Department. It was photographed at Tan-y-bwlch on 29 April 1989. *Author*

Below:
For many years the most important vehicle on the Festiniog Railway was the humble slate wagon. The oldest had timber frames — one survives in the museum. No 475, shown here in April 1989, is a replica constructed mainly of parts scavenged in Glan-y-mor yard at Boston Lodge. Behind it is No 2, an end-balcony brake van, converted from a Quarrymen's coach. The matchboard sides were restored in 1988. *Author*

Bottom:
At its peak there were over 1,000 iron-framed slate wagons on the railway. Many were scrapped to raise funds in the 1950s but enough survived for Boston Lodge-based volunteers to restore for a replica gravity train in the 1980s. By 1990 30 wagons had been restored and those responsible have ambitions to create a train of 50. The photograph shows a train of 17 slate wagons, many with loads of slate, and three bogie Hudsons, for extra braking power, approaching Tan-y-bwlch on 3 November 1986; the train had been pulled to Blaenau Ffestiniog by *Prince* and propelled back to Power Station Summit, near Tanygrisiau, before being released to return to Porthmadog by gravity. *Author*

III ORGANISATION AND PERSONNEL

29 The supervising personnel consists of the following:

    General Manager
    Traffic Superintendent & Secretary
    General Manager's clerk
    Accountant
    Loco Superintendent (and Manager of
Loco Carriage and Wagon Workshops.)
    (+ Works Foreman - added by hand)
Engineer and PW Inspector

30 General charges are 7.83% of the traffic receipts for 1920.

STATISTICS

31 The usual statistics are kept in order to render accounts required by the Accounts Act 1911, and those required by the Ministry of Transport.
Statistical Units or averages as kept by larger railways to show the results of Working of a number of trains or vehicles over different sections of a line calculated so as to shew such results in a single figure without recourse to a mass of detail, are not necessary to a management operating only 13½ miles of railway. Hence totals are more necessary than such unit statistics.

32 Also the conditions of gauge, working loads, gradients of the Festiniog Railway differ largely from those obtaining on other systems, and a comparison of train mile, ton mile, and vehicle mile costs with those of other Railways would be of little help.

33 The items of engine, shunting and pilotage mileage, the two latter calculated at 5 miles per hour under steam, <u>require monthly scrutiny</u> since the proportion of the second is undoubtedly excessive and the last noted entirely obtained from returns.

34 In the Locomotive Department it would appear necessary, especially in view of the possible extension of the system and the work demanded of the engines, to know exactly the capabilities of each engine, its 'mileage' life between general repairs, its coal consumption and the average life in service in months left in the group of nine engines.

35 Figures indicative of the life of an engine between General (or heavy repairs) have only recently been taken in hand, so that data over five years or so are not available.

39 The life of a Locomotive on the Festiniog Railway between General Repairs is said to be 15 months, this figure is not however given with reference to the mileage run, nor does it appear to be substantiated by figures.

40 No statistics are available whereby the life between General Repairs of the coaching and wagon stock may be known. For individual vehicles these figures are rarely kept since they involve much clerical labour.

41 Figures shewing the percentage of coaching vehicles and also wagons under general repairs for a number of years would be valuable in judging the personnel and equipment necessary in Loco, carriage and wagon workshops.

42 A certain number of complaints are on record from Quarry Managers concerning the shortage of empty wagons. It would appear to be most necessary to ascertain the average time spent by a slate wagon between its receipt over the weigh-bridges at Minffordd Junction. *(Sic)*
This would have to be averaged over a period of some months.

43 The number of Mineral wagons is approximately 1,200, deducting say 12½% undergoing general repairs 1,050 should be available for traffic.

    The daily demand appears to be as follows:

Llechwedd	30 per day per incline				x 2 =	60
Oakeley	60	"	"	"	"	x 2 =	120
Maenofferen							
	35	"	"	"	"	x 3 =	105
Votty	25	"	"	"	"	x 2 =	50
Rhiwbach	15	"	"	"	"	x 4 =	60
Brookes Quarry							
	15	"	"	"	"	x 2 =	30
							425

44 It would appear that either (a) wagons are kept under load for a disproportionate period or (b) remain in the quarries, or (c) are blocked in sidings as captives by full wagons coming in.

45 All three reasons would seem to apply. No demurrage charges are levied on wagons so that wagons remain in Quarry sidings or on Owners' Wharves under load for weeks. At Minffordd Junction the layout of the marshalling sidings rendered it most difficult to extract the empty wagons.

46 It appears impolitic to charge demurrage for wagons kept over three days in quarries or under load at wharves and it is said by the Management to be impossible to tender a statement of overdue wagons sent to the Quarries by individual wagon numbers so that owners may be advised....

47 It is observed that on certain quarry inclines that four empty wagons are handed over but two full wagons only received

owing to counter-balance difficulties on the inclines.

48 It is thought that this difficulty might be overcome by a suitable counter weight wagon kept for the purpose on the incline since the receipt of 4 empties for every 2 full wagons handed back to traffic is bound to lead to dislocation.

49 Should the result of the investigation mentioned in para 42 shew that less than 1,050 wagons are required to maintain the service the balance should be withdrawn from serving lines since their retention in service undoubtedly entails blocked sidings.

50 At the same time the provision of a relief siding in Minffordd yard fed from the Maenofferen yard by means of two turntables would undoubtedly relieve congestion and save shunting costs.

IV MAINTENANCE & RENEWAL OF WAY & WORKS

51 The following staff is employed:

PW Inspector	1
Sub Ganger and Labourers	10
Mason	1
Signal Fitter	1

54 The sub ganger and labourers, divided into 2 maintenance gangs, one working between Portmadoc and Cei Mawr (5m) and the other between Cei Mawr and Duffws. The main line mileage is approximately 13m 62c and the number of staff employed is therefore moderate.

57 The permanent way appears to be well maintained, but it must be remembered that the rails, with few exceptions, are old and worn.

62 Between Boston Lodge and Minffordd (about 1½ miles) the embankment is constantly subsiding, due to the blocking of a drain which carries water from a series of springs on the high side of the line. An attempt was made to pass this water through the bank at a high level, by means of a dam. The foundations of the dam are however faulty and the water is apparently finding its way through the Dam and under the Railway bank in an unauthorised channel....

63 The Girders of the Pont Newydd Bridge (Rhiw Plas) carrying the main road over the railway should be scaled and painted. The main girders have deteriorated through rust especially at the bearings.
The same remark applies to all the wrought steel and iron bridges on the system.

66 Some of the cuttings should be drained especially Lloc Meirig Farm. The sleepers will not last a tithe of their proper life unless this is attended to.

67 Ballast generally is very poor and insufficient.

68 The rail is generally speaking a 24 foot steel Double Head Rail about 41lbs per yard on 2 holed cast iron Chairs with 9 sleepers per rail.
There is also a 30ft rail with 11 sleepers per rail and a 50lb Steel Rail 30ft long which was laid recently. The chairs now being cast and put in use are 4 holed. All sharp curves are check railed.

71 Sleepers used consist of scotch fir, which have a very short life, oak which splits badly with the four holes through such a small section, and larch which lasts well.

72 Creosoted sleepers might be introduced with advantage.
There is no dating system, ie date headed nails driven into sleepers whereby the life and behaviour of sleepers can be ascertained with accuracy.

73 The wooden flooring of the girder bridges on the Dinas branch badly requires renewals, since being rotten they may cause accidents to workmen.

76 The main girders of Queens Bridge (Festiniog) require scaling and painting at an early date. Corrugated iron sheeted parapets on over bridges require attention. The batters of these might be tarred.

79 The Overhead structures are very low and gauges from which strings can be suspended, in order to warn brakesmen of the proximity of a low overhead structure, are now entirely bereft of such strings. This system appears to have been adopted on the advice of the Board of Trade, and any accident to brakesmen would call forth strictures from that Body.

V MAINTENANCE & RENEWALS OF ROLLING STOCK

80 The Company owns 9 steam locomotives:

Three, Fairlie double boiler, 4 wheel coupled, mounted on 2 bogies:

James Spooner	22 tons
Livingston Thompson	22 tons
Merddin Emrys	24 tons

One single boiler bogie, 4 wheeled coupled:

Taliesin	17 tons

Five, Tank engines with tenders, 4 wheeled coupled:

Little Giant	13 tons
Welsh Pony	13 tons
Prince	12 tons

Princess		12 tons	
Palmerston		12 tons	

Coaching Vehicles

	Nos	1st	3rd
Carriage of uniform class	16	48	232
Composite Carriages	6	76	224
Workmen's Carriages	33	—	396
Luggage Parcel & brake	5		
Carriage Trucks	1		
	61		

Merchandise & Mineral Wagons

Open Wagons	1,215
Covered Wagons	13
Rail and Timber Wagons	19
Brake Vans	2
	1,249

81 The three double engines are in good condition the last named having recently been reboilered.

The single boilered engine *Taliesin* is now undergoing heavy repairs, and in any case does not appear to be fit for heavy work.
82 A new boiler has recently been fixed in *Prince*, whilst *Princess* is now in the shops awaiting a new boiler. *Palmerston* has been lent on hire. (To the Vale of Rheidol Railway in 1912 — hire charge £2 a day, 1913, 1914 — hire charge £22 per week for two weeks and £2 a day thereafter, 1915, 1921 and 1922 — hire charge £2 10 0 a day.)
83 Three of the nine engines are in process of general repairs a high proportion, explained by the fact that 1912 and 1913 were years of depression in the slate trade and necessary repairs were not, therefore, undertaken as required.

VI LOCOMOTIVE CARRIAGE AND WAGON WORKSHOPS

84 The weekly wages bill of the above is as follows:

Supervision staff, Loco Superintendent & Clerical Staff

47½%		£5	19	6

a Stationary Engine Driver and Boiler attendant

(Supply power to Shops)	1	£3	3	7
b Yard Labourer & Saw Mill	1½	£3	17	1
c Foundry	2	£4	19	10
d Smithy	5	£14	10	8
e Fitting Shop	7	£16	19	8
f Carpenters' Shop	2	£6	18	10
g Paint Shop	1	£3	11	5
		£60	0	7

91 The personnel employed in the workshops has increased from <u>21 in 1913 to 36 in 1920</u>; a certain amount of work is done for outside Clients, such as the Quarry masters, mostly foundry work, geared wheels, incline rollers etc.

During 1917 Total Profit on work done	£85
During 1918 Total Profit on work done	£199
During 1919 Total Profit on work done	£258
During 1920 Total Profit on work done	£66

It must be remembered however that 1913 was a year of depression in the slate trade and renewals and repairs were kept low.
92 The Lighting of the workshop is effected by means of oil lamps which appear to be most inadequate.

V LOCOMOTIVE RUNNING EXPENSES

93 Locomotive running expenses were 32.94% of receipts in 1920.

Below:
Tan-y-bwlch Station Mistress, Bessie Jones, approaches *Palmerston* in 1935. Judging by the length of it, it is unlikely that the train was very profitable, even when the milk had been taken on board. *R. E. Tustin Collection*

The present weekly cost of the Locomotive Running Shed is:

Loco Supt and Clerical Staff 20%		£ 2	12	0	
('?£12/12/0' added by hand)					
Drivers	6)				
Stokers	6)	£47	3	7	
Cleaners	5	£10	13	0	
Coalmen	1½	£ 4	12	10	
Fitters	2	£ 6	17	10	
		£71	19	3	

94 With two shunting engines constantly employed, and two train Engines working from 5.30 to 10.7pm, the number of employees in the Running Shed cannot be reduced. During the winter months 2 Drivers, 2 Stokers, and 1 cleaner are dispensed with.

VI COAL CONSUMPTION

95 The Coal consumption of the double ended Fairlie type engines, is normally about 45½lbs per mile, that of the tender engine type (*Little Giant* & *Welsh Pony* & *Prince* class) 23lbs per mile.

96 In July 1921 owing to poor Coal received during the coal dispute, the average consumption per mile rose to as much as 54.16lbs for the first, and 25lb for the second.

97 The cost of Lubricants, engine Oil, Cylinder oil, tallow and waste &c per engine and per vehicle mile, is not recorded except as lump issues in the stores ledger. It would appear to be helpful in checking waste and unnecessary expenditure if statistics of the cost of lubrication were kept and compared with the cost of lubrication per mileage run from month to month and with the records obtained on other railways.

VII TRAFFIC EXPENSES

98 The expenses under this head were 43.55% of receipts in 1920.

FESTINIOG RAILWAY - TRAFFIC STAFF AT EACH STATION

VIII PASSENGER SAFETY AND SIGNALLING

100 The Festiniog Railway has not been brought under the designation of 'Light Railway' and does not come under the Light Railway Act.

101 Under the act of 1868, a light railway is defined as one when the load does not exceed 8 tons on any pair of wheels and where the speed does not exceed 25mph.

102 Neither the Axle loads nor the speed on the Festiniog Railway exceed these 'minimum' and under the working of the Light Railway Act of 1896 59-60 Vict C48 Section 18, the Board of Trade may authorise the working as a light railway any existing or authorised railway.

105 The Festiniog Railway is controlled under the special rules and regulations of 1876 as approved by the Board of Trade. As a passenger line whereon passenger trains are crossed, block signalling is legally enforced under the act of 1889.

106 It would appear that an order to treat the Festiniog Railway as a light Railway, would not have the effect of cheapening operation.

108 There are 12 stopping places in the 13m 18c of the line including the termini, of which 11 are block stages, and fitted with the electric staff, with the exception of 5 sections which retain the staff and ticket system as follows:

109

0	Portmadoc	Electric Staff Instrument
1m 0	Boston Lodge	" " "
2m 23	Minffordd	" " "
		& staff & ticket
3m 37	Penrhyndeudraeth	
		Staff and Ticket
7m 41	Tanybwlch	Electric Staff Instrument

FESTINIOG RAILWAY - TRAFFIC STAFF AT EACH STATION

Station-master	Clerks	Pass Guards	Goods Guards	Porters	Signalmen	Gate Keepers	Oilmen	Shunters
Portmadoc	1	3			4(1) A 1 Parcel			1
Boston Lodge						2		
Minffordd & Weigh Office	1	(1)3			2		1	
Penrhyndeudraeth	1				1	1		
Tanybwlch	1				1			
Tunnel					1			
Tanygrisiau	1				1			
Blaenau Jct		1				2		1 Also acts as porter
Duffws	1	1	1	2	1	4(1)		1 1

A — 2 Porters act as Guard daily for 5 & 6 hours respectively.   (1) Porter does the work of pointsman & oilman for part of each day

			& staff & ticket
9	61	Dduallt	Halt no block stage
11	0	Moelwyn Halt	Halt no block stage
11	54	Tanygrisiau	Electric Staff
			instrument
12	56	Glan-y-pwll	Box No 3
			Electric Staff
			instrument
			& staff and ticket
12	68	Blaenau Festiniog (L&NWR)	
			Staff & Ticket
		(GWR) Box No 2	
			" "
13	18	Duffws Box No 1	
			" "

110 The siting of the loco carriage and wagon workshops 1 mile from Portmadoc, and the fact that all engines leave the workshops, running shed or turntable over the main line, necessitated the establishment of a cabin between Portmadoc and Minffordd Junction, to control the workshop running shed and turntable points.

110 Normally engine facilities are sited within station limits so that attachment and detachment to trains does not block a main line.

111 The Portmadoc end of the line is signalled by old fashioned disc signals, worked from a quadrant arm. The signals at the Dinas end being of the modern semaphore type.

112 It is noted that certain signals are so counter weighted as to show 'off' (safety) should a wire break or a pin be removed. <u>Such signals may lead to collisions.</u>

113 The <u>Festiniog area not only possesses three passenger platforms but three signal cabins, within a distance of half</u> a mile.

116 The line between Dinas Junction and Duffws contains two parallel tracks, the intention being that one should be utilised as a siding for mineral traffic and the other as main line. Owing however to the subsequent situation of Blaenau Festiniog passenger platform the position of the mineral and main line have been reversed.

117 The sharp curvature of the line between No 1 and No 3 Box whereby all signals controlled cannot be seen, necessitates the establishment of a box at No 2.

IX POTENTIALITIES FOR INCREASED BUSINESS

118 EQUIPMENT

The Railway is well equipped with engine power, coaching and goods vehicles, signalling etc and should be capable of carrying a very large increase of traffic both passenger and goods.

119 GOODS TRAFFIC

(Refer para 8) Outside the slate and roadstone traffic no great expansion can be looked for, except perhaps in the coal traffic, which will quicken with the advent of winter and cheaper coal.

120 The opening of the district Co-operative Stores at Penrhyndeudraeth will provide a small increase in merchandise. *(On the platform, now the living room and kitchen of the Volunteers' Hostel.)*

121 The Quarries at the Moelwyn Halt and the Festiniog Granite Co appear to be expanding concerns and should continue to expand their tonnage.

122 It is stated that the Moelwyn Mines are about to reopen.

123 MINERAL TRAFFIC

The output of slates from the five Quarries situated at Blaenau Festiniog, will probably not increase as fast as the present demand for slates would indicate, since owing to a pre-war depression in the slate trade, a large amount of 'spade work' now has to be done per ton of slates quarried.

124 The foreign trade in slates, a former source of affluence to the Festiniog Railway, is now dormant owing to adverse exchange. A revival in this trade would give the Festiniog Railway the long haul to Portmadoc in place of the short distance to the L&NWR & GWR trans-shipment stations at Festiniog.

PASSENGER TRAFFIC *(para 21 - added by hand)*

127 The normal passenger traffic should shew a very small increase following the development of the Quarries, but no great

Above right:
Down passenger in the woods between the wars. *Author's Collection*

Right:
Shown on the link line to the Welsh Highland Railway in August 1930, *Prince's* cab and tank lining are clearly seen. Remnants of this red/lined cream livery were found when the green paint was stripped from the cabsides during the rebuild completed in 1980. The weights in front of the smokebox show that recent difficulties in keeping the front of this locomotive bearing on the rails are no new phenomenon — similar extra weight was added to the front of the locomotive in 1988, following the discovery of frame cracks caused by uneven weight distribution. *Collection FR Heritage Group*

increase of resident population may be expected.

TOURIST TRAFFIC It is considered however that a very large tourist traffic may be built up, during the Summer months May to August.

X POTENTIALITIES FOR INCREASED BUSINESS

128 As far as may be ascertained from foreign bookings such holiday centres as Rhyl, Colwyn Bay, Llandudno are as yet untapped, since the bookings for August 1921 have been entirely local or from nearer holiday centres as Criccieth and Pwllheli.

129 The Motor charabanc is a rival competitor which though powerful cannot compete with the cheaper fares of the railway, nor can it approximate the 'turn over' or carrying capacity of the railway.

131 The extraordinary 'intimacy' of the railway running, at an elevation of several hundreds of feet above the road, with every bend and turn in the mountainside, provides the sightseer with ever changing vista of moorland, bare rocky escarpments, and far below the silver ribbon of the river winding through the golden estuary sands to the open sea beyond.

133 It is thought that a tour commencing at Rhyl, Llandudno &c up the Conway Valley to Festiniog, down the Festiniog Railway to Portmadoc, with an hour or so halt at Portmadoc, would be cheaper and more interesting, than that providing for return via Afonwen Jct with its change of trains and tedious journey lacking in scenic interest.

134 Cheap refreshments should be provided at the top terminal, and perhaps at Tan-y-bwlch, with opportunity for consumption 'en route'.

The tourist who cannot afford charabanc tours cannot afford hotels and hotel prices, but must have facilities for refreshments if the trip is to be popularised.

135 As remarked in para 91 a certain amount of work has been under taken in the past by the railway loco carriage and wagon workshop for clients outside the Company, mostly quarry masters.

There is obviously a large amount of such work offering and the Railway owning as it does a large amount of scrap should be able to compete most effectively for such work, as incline rollers, geared wheels, tip wagon wheels &c.

The Company also owns a large number of patterns of castings employed in quarries. There is however a locally owned workshop and foundry in Portmadoc which can and does obtain orders from quarry masters, at prices with which the Railway workshops cannot compete.

This is explained by the fact that the family owning these workshops do not charge their own personal labour at union rates.

136 The following criticisms are made of the general working of the Company's Workshops.

1 The disproportionate number of apprentices employed in the fitting shops. It is considered that two skilled fitters will give more remunerative services than the five apprentices shewn in para 84e and 88a c and be cheaper. It is considered that these shops are not large enough to carry so many apprentices.

2 The Carpenters spend a large <u>amount of time in planing which</u> is done in all modern shops by planing machine.

3 A great waste of time is entailed in lifting carriage (sic) and wagons off their bogie trucks by means of jacks and packing. No <u>overhead</u> power <u>exists for this</u> purpose. A five ton crane would suffice.

4 Men constantly break off a machining job &c to assist in lifting wheels &c onto the wheel lathe. A 6 or 7 cwt hand pushed (Herbert Morris) crane trolley would obviate this.

5 The lighting of the workshops during the winter is most deficient and expensive in maintenance, being by means of oil lamps. It is obvious that little or no accurate work can be turned out under such conditions of lighting.

An oil engine with battery and about 30 lamps are all that is required, or if cheaper, acetylene generating plant.

6 Heavy engine repairs are carried out in the running shed, but machining &c in the loco workshops. Consequently <u>there is time lost in unnecessary walking to and fro</u>.

7 The work done in the foundry which appears excellent, is however much prejudiced by the absence of moulding boxes of sufficient capacity and size, nor can much work offered by quarry masters be undertaken at times for this reason.

X RAILWAY EXTENSIONS

138 The little seaside resort Borth-y-Gest village is yearly becoming more popular with visitors. An extension of the railway to serve Borth-y-Gest has been surveyed but

entails either a heavy rock cutting or a tunnel. The distance is only about 1 mile but it is unlikely that the extension may show any return on the capital involved.

XI PROPOSALS AND OBSERVATIONS

158 Referring to abstract No 10 of 1913 and of 1920. The following is a comparison of the tonnage and passengers carried.

	1913	1920
Passengers	132,481	117,843
Goods and Minerals	88,961	78,829
Train Miles (Loaded)	60,928	57,372
Engine Miles	74,409	77,989
Engine Shunting miles & Light &c	13,366	19,074

159 In 1913 there were more loaded (or remunerative) train miles run than in 1920, but the number of engine miles in 1913 was less than that of 1920. This is accounted for by the fact that more full unengined slate trains were run, which would appear to be the case from the goods and mineral mileage. With more slate trains run a larger shunting mileage in 1913 than in 1920 would be expected, but the reverse is the case. The amount of slate tonnage has decreased by 11% in 1920 but the amount of shunting incurred to marshall (sic) and sort that tonnage has increased 44%.

160 The 8 hour day does not seem a complete explanation for this, since slate trains and shunting wagons therefore can well remain in the 8 hour day.

161 Working expenses in 1913 were 74.04% of receipts whilst in 1920 they had risen to 160.18% of receipts.

162 It is obvious that no business can be carried on for long with such results, and that whatever the reasons be adduced such as the introduction of the minimum wages and the 8 hour day &c, a drastic remedy is necessary to preserve the life of the railway.

163 This is a problem which is exercising the mind of every railwayman today, and it is obvious that there is no golden rule whereby revenue and expenditure may be equalised applicable alike to all systems, and that every Railway administration must work out its own salvation by experiment and deductions therefrom.

164 It is also obvious that in order to make such experiments the management must be given a defined policy to work on and that no phase or result in the working of that policy should be deemed too insignificant for report and comment.

165 The Staff employed on the maintenance and renewal of ways and works are not excessive, the usual allowance on certain railways being 1 per mile, but in such cases there are no station staff and the nearest permanent Way Gangman, are present at stations as and when called for by telephone to assist in hand shunting or handling road side goods that may be required.

166 The Staff employed on the maintenance and renewal of locomotives &c do not appear to be excessive (with the exception of the large number of apprentices employed) for if the Loco Carriage and Wagon Workshops are required every department must be manned.

167 The staff employed on traffic running does not appear excessive, excepting the number of clerks employed at Minffordd and the Oilman at Blaenau Junction. For if 5 passenger stations with a frequent passenger train service over 16½ hours daily is required on the line then the staff and relieving staff to man these stations is also required under present day conditions of labour.

168 An order might possibly be obtained to replace the level crossing gates at Minffordd and Penrhyndeudraeth by cattle guards but the present gate keepers, one being a Pensioner and the other a woman are inexpensive. (Minffordd Crossing was automated in 1991.)

169 The signalman at the tunnel Mile 11 is perhaps extravagant; if dispensed with his Tunnel duties should be taken over by the Permanent Way Gangman who would be required to examine the tunnel twice daily on his outward and homeward journey. The siding points at Moelwyn Halt are locked by a key on the electric staff and cannot be moved or left open by error for the key cannot be withdrawn if open, and the driver cannot proceed without the Staff.

170 The locomotive running staff cannot be said to be excessive having regard to the 16½ hour timetable under the 8 hour day rule.

171 The maintenance of Locomotive Carriage and Wagon Workshops are an expenditure out of all proportion to the mileage and stock of the railway.

173 In order therefore that the Workshops may pay their way they must either undertake a very large amount of outside work or must be run as a separate undertaking, with a Contract for rolling stock repairs for the Festiniog Company.

Above:
After 1923 the England locomotives regularly worked on the Welsh Highland Railway; here *Little Giant* is seen at Dinas Junction. There can be no question about ownership, the photograph shows the FR crest on the cabside and the monogram on the tender. *Loco Pub Co*

Top:
Following a period out of use, awaiting either a new boiler or repairs to that existing, *Livingston Thompson* returned to service in 1932 bearing the name *Taliesin*, the earlier locomotive of that name having then been withdrawn; the boiler had been sent to Bristol for repairs which included fitting a new firebox. The vehicle next to the locomotive in this 1930s view is No 2, rebuilt in 1921 with a new body which included two passenger compartments as well as the guard's van; it is now numbered 10.
D. W. K. Jones Robert Humm Collection

174 As mentioned in Para 135, there is a firm established in Portmadoc, who are able to underquote the Railway <u>workshops but it is possible that interests might be amalgamated in a construction and repair Company.</u>

175 The reduction of traffic expenses which have risen from 20½% of receipts between the years 1913 and 1917 might be effected under three alternative proposals.

1 The Reduction of the passenger train service

2 Introducing a shuttle train system either in part or wholly.

3 Extension or lengthening the existing block sections.

ALTERNATIVE 1

It would appear to be a good Opportunity both as regards the travelling public, staff &c are concerned to make such reduction for the forthcoming winter and review matters again in the light of experience in June 1922.

176 It is suggested that a service of the following nature be run. The Timetable *(not shown)* being illustrative only and would provide for a daily goods service. 3 up and 3 down passenger including workmens trains and two down unengined slate trains.

A shunting engine would work the Portmadoc and Minffordd yards within 8 hours daily, and the engine taking the workmens train up would do the Duffws Shunting and about 12 hours work daily, as would No 2 Engine working the daily goods and passenger train.

179 The double ended engines are not allowed over the road bridge between the Wharf Sidings and the Station by the Owners of the bridge (The Tremadoc Estate) nor does the clearance between the walls in these sidings permit of the movement of these engines.

180 Moreover Minffordd Junction is entered by a sharp curve on the steep gradient and the double engines cannot safely negotiate this curve. Moreover the shunting of Minffordd yard occupies some hours daily, which the road engines could not spare.

181 The shunting at Portmadoc into the various Wharf sidings could doubtless be carried out by means of a horse, but a horse could not negotiate the steep incline into Minffordd Junction with more than 2 or 3 wagons at a time and the work would never be completed.

ALTERNATIVE NO 2

181 Certain Railways are worked entirely with a shuttle service ie with only one engine in steam. Such railways dispense with the necessity of signals, block instruments and station staff. Stations become stopping places, booking is done on the train by means of the punch ticket method. A key (generally Annetts) is carried by the driver as authority to proceed, which key unlocks all sidings off the main line, this key cannot be withdrawn unless points are set again correctly for the main line.

182 The introduction of this system to the Festiniog line would eventually entail the alteration of the coaching stock to provide a gangway down the centre, which should not be a difficult matter.

204 The <u>third alternative</u> proposal is as follows:

1 Adoption of the ticket punch method of booking on the train.

2 Close the following stations except as halts:

Penrhyndeudraeth

Tanygrisiau

By removing the Station Staff, locking the sidings with a key attached to electrical staff, lengthening the block sections accordingly, and blinding the existing signals.

3 Close Duffws Station to passenger booking and transfer the booking to Blaenau Festiniog and book interchange passengers only as far as the GWR Station. Local goods could be booked at Duffws at stated hours only.

4 Passenger trains will not run through to Duffws except as empty brakes and Box No 1 will be no longer necessary. Points may then be handlevered and worked from the ground.

206 Under alternatives 1 and 3 the Signal Box at Boston Lodge, which controls the running shed, cannot be dispensed with, without the construction of a siding from that point to Portmadoc Station yard clear of the running road, and a costly deviation of the main line to the back of the running shed. *('? store shed & works' added by hand)*

207 Alternatives 2 and 3 would of course require the sanction and approval of the Board of Trade.

The adoption of alternative 2 would shew the greatest saving in operating costs, but would involve a certain amount of dislocation to existing working.

208 It would appear therefore that the adoption of alternative No 3 *('?No 1' also*

added by hand) primarily with a view to obtaining experience and the subsequent adoption of alternative No 2 would be the wisest course.

Writing to the General Manager, Frederick Vaughan, on 12 September 1921, seeking further information required for the completion of his report, Spring concluded by thanking Vaughan and his staff for 'kindness & courtesy (shown) to me during my sojourn on your railway' and said, 'I am afraid I have discovered nothing that was not fully known before'. Spring effectively gave the new Board a manual, or a lecture, on how to run a railway, though his comments on signalling and operating did betray his military background and lack of experience in the real world. Apart from his confusion with the geography, Spring was also mistaken about the indiscriminate use of wagons (paragraph 18) — the three-tonners would not pass on some inclines — and fishplate replacement (paragraph 70) — it was the fishbellied type (Spooner & Huddart Patent) which were being replaced. His comment on recording fuel consumption (paragraph 34) demonstrates the decline since the Spooner years, when coal consumption was calculated to two decimal places. Spring's comment on paragraph 112 was certainly understated; what he was describing was illegal!

Unfortunately the Board took notice of very little of the report so far as operation of the railway was concerned. They did, however, introduce catering to Tan-y-bwlch (and got the Station Mistress to meet the trains wearing Welsh national dress), close Duffws station and reduce Penrhyn and Tanygrisiau stations to halt status. They also fatally misunderstood his remarks about locomotive maintenance, assuming he meant that repairs were being carried out too often instead of taking too long. At least they didn't introduce his 'shuttle' system of train working, surely a disaster in the making had it been implemented.

The Festiniog Railway (Light Railway) Order of 1923 was also a response to Spring's report. It authorised the railway to be worked as a light railway, with the consequent savings on signalling. It also allowed the company 'to construct light railways at Portmadoc forming a junction with the light railways referred to in the Welsh Highland Railway (Light Railway) Order, 1922', the construction of a new station 'in substitution for the present Portmadoc Station of the Company', and amended the borrowing powers.

During the 1920s the number of passengers carried was increased by tourists seeking to view the remote scenic splendours visible from the 'Toy Railway' or 'Faery Line', as the company promoted itself, whilst they passed through the Vale of Ffestiniog. The company saw the value of this traffic and published many handbills and posters offering a variety of excursions which included travel on the railway. In July 1922 a 20 page *Programme of Excursion Facilities from Festiniog Railway Stations and Time Table* offered everything from 3rd class holiday season tickets (7s 6d, [37.5p] for seven days) on the FR, to cheap day and weekend tickets to both the Cambrian and North Wales coasts and day trips to Bala, Corwen and Llangollen. The timetable even offered a Parliamentary train (5.15am from Portmadoc, arrive Duffws 6.15am, depart Duffws 7.00am, arrive Portmadoc 7.58am) and the overtime-incurring evening trains (9.00pm from Portmadoc, 9.10pm from Duffws) on Wednesdays, Thursdays and Saturdays. A journey on the Railway was described thus:

The Festiniog Railway (13.5 miles in length) commences at Portmadoc and terminates at Duffws. It has a gradual and continuous ascent the whole way, attaining an elevation of upwards of 700 feet above sea level. The following are some of the points of interest to be seen in taking a trip to Duffws:

In crossing the estuary of the river Glaslyn immediately after leaving Portmadoc (looking to the left facing engine), a good view is obtained of the Snowdonian Range, Moelwyn, Cynicht (sic), Moel Hebog and other mountains, also of the Vale of Madoc and the well-known Tremadoc Rocks. On the right is a view of the open sea and Borthygest.

The next Station is Minffordd (2½ miles). This is the junction with the Cambrian Railways, and passengers to and from that railway change here. After leaving this station, good views of Moelwyn and Cynicht (left), Merionethshire Mountains and Harlech Castle (right), are to be had. Tea and light refreshments are supplied at Minffordd Station.

Penrhyndeudraeth is the next station (1½ miles). The view of Merionethshire Mountains and Harlech Castle is still to be seen, also the charming Vale of Maentwrog and the windings of the river Dwyryd. On approaching the next station, Tanybwlch (4 miles) there is a good view of the Vale of Festiniog and of the villages of Maentwrog and Festiniog. From Tanybwlch Station tourists usually visit the Raven and Rhayadr Ddu Waterfalls and make the ascent of Moelwyn. Tea and light refreshments may be had at the station.

The next station is Dduallt (2½ miles) from which the beautiful Falls of Cymmerau may be visited (about 1½ miles from the station). The Vales of Maentwrog and Festiniog as well as the river Dwyryd are also to be seen between Tanybwlch and Dduallt.

From Tanygrisiau the next station (2 miles) another and good ascent of Moelwyn can be made. There is an easy route by the road leading past Cwmorthin Lake and the Rhosydd Quarry, thence by a path to the summit. The Moelwyn Range, though not so high as that of Snowdon, is considered by some to surpass it in picturesque beauty, and the view from the summit is magnificent. The Cymmerau Waterfalls and Roman Bridge can also be visited from Tanygrisiau.

The next station is Blaenau Festiniog. Passengers for Bettwsycoed, Llandudno, and other stations on the L&NW Railway, change at Blaenau Festiniog, the L&NW station being within a few yards. Blaenau Festiniog is in the midst of the far-famed Festiniog Slate Quarries, and surrounded by the Manod and Moelwyn Ranges. Through the courtesy of the Quarry Proprietors, arrangements have been made whereby tourists can visit the Quarries. Within a two-minutes run the train reaches the Junction Station where passengers for the Great Western Railway change for Bala &c. The terminus of the Line is at Duffws (next station) from which passengers during the summer months are conveyed to to Festiniog and Cynfael Waterfalls and other places of interest.

Notice that there was no mention of the two tunnels, obviously for fear of frightening off prospective passengers! An undated (but available at the Manchester office of the Cambrian Railways and in 1914 Oswestry requested more for Birmingham and Liverpool) four-colour leaflet revealed that the quarries open to tourists were the premises of the Oakley Slate Quarries Co Ltd and Messrs J. W. Greaves & Sons Ltd, where a sight of 'Block Splitting and making of Slates' was promised. Now known more commonly as Gloddfa Ganol and Llechwedd respectively, these quarries still receive many of their visitors via the Festiniog Railway.

In 1923 the Welsh Highland Railway was opened from Portmadoc to Dinas, near Caernarvon, via Aberglaslyn and Beddgelert, a distance of 22 miles. It was never successful and closed on 31 December 1933. The FR took a lease on its neighbour and operated a summer service during the following three years, though with no greater success. At the end of the 1936 season the line was closed for good, the company having been in the hands of a receiver since 1927.

From 1923, until he died in 1931, the Festiniog came under the influence of the light railway king, Col Holman Fred Stephens. The Colonel was well known for the ramshackle collection of minor railways he ran — with varying degrees of success — from an office in Tonbridge, Kent. In addition to being a member of the FR board, he was also appointed Engineer, Managing Director, Locomotive Superintendent and Company Chairman at various times, some of them concurrently! Stephens was also simultaneously involved with the Welsh Highland Railway. Unfortunately his rather brusque approach was not well received by spirited Welsh railwaymen and the two sides rarely, if ever, agreed on the best way of achieving the desired result. To reduce costs he did introduce the internal combustion engine to the FR, acquiring two ex-World War 1 locomotives for shunting purposes in 1923 and 1925. Now known as *Moelwyn* and *Mary Ann*, both still exist.

The tourist traffic was also to decline during the 1930s, despite continued efforts to attract new business, including the painting of carriages in different colours. In 1935 the company did try to make it easier for the less affluent to use the railway by converting one of the cottages at Boston Lodge to be a ramblers' hostel. Despite a promotional leaflet and advertising in the *Liverpool Echo* and relevant handbooks it did not re-open in 1936.

The centenary in 1936 was a very low key affair, with Robert Evans, the Manager, making a radio broadcast on the BBC on 12 December; Fox Photos sent a photographer to Tan-y-bwlch on 9 December, 'in order to synchronise release with our London office prior to the broadcast'. Previously, in September, a photographer from Hoylake had also taken photographs to release to the press.

In 1938 the Great Western Railway was offering 'Cheap day return tickets over the Festiniog Toy Railway (13½ miles of enchanting scenery)' from Machynlleth and Cambrian Coast stations to Minffordd. From Towyn the fare to Tan-y-bwlch ('for Beautiful Vale of MAENTWROG, Waterfalls and ASCENT OF MOELWYN') was 5/- (25p) and to Blaenau ('For the Slate Quarries'), 5/8d (28½p). Betws-y-coed was also an advertised option via this route. Engine failures, due to reduced maintenance, could easily make travel on the 'Faery Line' a journey of epic proportions, with missed connections with the standard-gauge links commonplace. Meanwhile, the quarrymen took to the buses.

The old Festiniog Railway management did not rate its quarrymen passengers very highly, which may have had something to do with the quarrymen only making two journeys on the railway each week for a good number of years — up to the quarries on Monday morning and back again on Saturday lunchtime; perhaps the railway considered that the return on investment for the necessary rolling stock was insufficient to warrant more than the most basic facilities. Only two accounts are known describing a journey on the quarrymen's train, one of them by a quarryman. Written by James Parry, it was published in *Caban*, the Oakeley Quarry house magazine, in 1960, its writing inspired by the Festiniog Railway revival.

The Romance and Pleasure of the 'Trên Bach'

In an article giving an account of a first journey on the 'trên bach' (little train) from Porthmadog to Blaenau Ffestiniog it is quite reasonable for you to expect to read about the incomparable beauty of the Maentwrog Valley, of the splendid view looking towards the Cader Idris or the natural, oil painting quality of the scene coming alive as you pass Tafarn Trip Lake, Tan-y-bwlch.

But, looking back on my own first journey on the railway, coming up with my father to work in the quarry, I must admit that it is not the splendour of nature that first springs to mind. I doubt very much if you would expect that in the reminiscences of a 16-year old youth, when you consider that he had been woken at three in the morning to walk six miles to Porthmadog station and had then travelled in darkness throughout the journey!

The first picture that comes to mind when I recollect that particular journey is of a group of about a dozen men walking to the train, each carrying a 'wallet' over his shoulder. This was a sort of white bag, similar to a pillow case, in which were carried the groceries which would provision him during the week at the quarry barracks. The middle part of the 'wallet' would go over one shoulder with the contents divided evenly on either side — one part in front, the other over the back as a counterbalance. Each end of the 'wallet' would be tied under the armpits. You would usually find butter, a dozen eggs, home-baked bread, a cake and a pound of bacon in each bag.

I can remember walking towards the little train as it stood resembling a row of chicken huts in the gloom, and after buying a ticket — known as the 'white ticket' — I stepped inside the dim carriage. There was room for about six to sit at each end and between the two doors there stood something that resembled an inverted bathtub known as the 'mule'. Each man had his chosen seat. Being a newcomer I had to sit on the mule.

As we left Porthmadog the train was fairly empty but a good many joined us at Penybwlch (Penrhyn) so that it became full. At Penrhyn a man came to sit beside me. His name was Bob Pritchard. At first glance I didn't particularly take to him. To be honest — I didn't like the look of of him, but as time went by I came to know him as one of the most pleasant men I ever met. First impressions do not always count for the better!

Looking around me on the train I noticed a number of chalk crosses on the partition above some of the seats, one or two above others and none at all above some. I concluded that this must be a secret sign to mark men's seats — the actual number of crosses saving people from having to write their names out in full. I didn't have to travel for very long to realise that my guess was wrong and for the correct solution to dawn on me. Let me explain. If someone told a suspect tale a cross would be placed above the teller. A lie would deserve two crosses and a white lie the ultimate three crosses.

Although it started off in the early hours both summer and winter there were no heating facilities on the train and neither were there any lights. Rather than suffer the cold and darkness each traveller had his own way of making the journey more comfortable. The carriage would be lit by means of a 'snyffyn' — a short piece of candle stuck to the partition by means of a lump of clay and, at great risk safety-wise, warmth was achieved by burning paper on the carriage floor.

At each stop the carriage doors were carefully locked but I soon saw that most men had their own keys to open doors as and when they wished. These keys were either inherited from former workers or were made by quarry blacksmith Huw Price.

The main purpose of the keys was to allow the men to jump off the train just before it arrived at the station so as to spare them having to walk back towards home. If you stood on the platform at Penybwlch station when the quarrymen's train was approaching you would notice almost all the doors opening before the train came into the platform. Half-bodies and legs would stick out stiffly as the men made ready to jump as they came in line with certain steps and stairs which led to the road. The train would arrive at the station with its doors waving like wings and the guard, without any fuss or complaint, would walk along the platform closing and locking doors before signalling the driver to resume the journey. After some practice many of the men became quite accomplished in the art of jumping off trains.

Those working in the Oakeley and Llechwedd Quarries got off the train at 'Stesion Fain' (Narrow Station, opposite the ex-L&NWR standard-gauge station) and I remember one daring passenger in particular, who decided that he would jump off before reaching the station so that he could be the first to reach the barracks that day. Steam swirled everywhere as he jumped. I recollect him stopping rather abruptly and we got off to find that he had jumped into one of the station supports which he had not seen due to the misty steam which had enveloped everywhere. He did not reach barracks before any of the others.

Saturday (mid-day) arrived on that first week at work in the quarry and I saw the little train for the first time in proper light. The journey home was far more pleasant for all of us. In the height of summer it was always a delight to travel up through Tan-y-bwlch woodlands in the morning light.

In winter we met with many adventures travelling up on the little railway. I remember the train coming to a very sudden halt once — the reason being that a tree had fallen across the track. Some of the men had to get off to manhandle it onto the side. Another time a snow drift had blocked a cutting. It was eventually cleared by the train reversing, picking up speed and bulldozing its way through.

A book could be written on the interesting stories relating to both passengers and train but I shall only mention one more. Visitors would sometimes travel with the workers in summer. I remember one particular Monday morning when such a visitor got on our train and set next to Tomos Williams, 'Tobi' as he was known locally because he had once been in the service of a Mr Toby of Criccieth. I recall that Tobi was in a rather drowsy state for most of the

journey and he soon became impatient with the visitor who kept describing the scenery along certain stretches and relating stories associated with some of them. All this was well known to Tobi and his fellow travellers. The train halted at Dduallt station. Looking at the lake close to the station the visitor remarked to Tobi:

'Did you know that they say that there is no bottom to that lake?'

Tobi opened one eye in a cold stare.

'Well,' he sighed, 'how the hell is it that it holds water, then?'

The stranger remained silent for the remainder of the journey.

The Festiniog's passenger service was withdrawn 12 days after the outbreak of war in 1939. Slate trains continued to run as required, and when motive power was available, throughout the war. Of the nine locomotives reported on in 1915, only *Princess* and *Merddin Emrys* were in service in 1939; *James Spooner* had been condemned in 1933, *Livingston Thompson* was under repair, *Little Giant* had been withdrawn in 1932, *Prince* had been out of service since 1937, *Palmerston* was providing steam for a mechanical hammer at Boston Lodge and *Taliesin* had been dismantled since 1932. The Welsh Highland Railway's single Fairlie *Moel Tryfan* had come into Festiniog ownership in 1937 but was also in a dismantled state. Strangely, the money was found to obtain a new boiler for *Prince* but it remained unfitted after delivery in 1945.

After the war it quickly became clear that there were no funds, either within the company or elsewhere, to bring the track and rolling stock to a safe operating condition. So on 1 August 1946 the Festiniog Railway was abruptly closed. Powers to close the line legally could only be had by spending money the company did not have, to promote an Act of Parliament — the legislation required was not enacted until 1962; section 83 of the Transport Act of that year applies (and was used to abandon formally the 28 chains of the old route between Dduallt and the old Moelwyn Tunnel in 1991). Everything was left to rot, or to be vandalised, where it stood.

Almost immediately attempts were made by outsiders to find ways of re-opening the railway, possibly using volunteers to assist a nucleus of paid staff. Eight years were to pass before all the legal and financial obstacles were overcome and a group of people including Alan Pegler, provider of the necessary financial support, was able to obtain a controlling shareholding. Right from the start the new board was supported by the newly formed Festiniog Railway Society.

Dduallt

Below:
Dduallt is the most remote station on the Festiniog Railway, nine miles from Portmadoc and having no road access. The lake, Rhoslyn, is now increasingly overgrown. The train in this 1887 photograph is the same as that illustrated at Minffordd, headed by *James Spooner. R. H. Bleasdale*

Bottom:
Dduallt became, in 1968, the next terminal for the revived FR. Since 1963 it had been the site of the first steps taken to build a deviation route to Tanygrisiau; the station was to become much more formal than that photographed on 11 August 1958. The footbridge, left centre, marks the location of the present rail bridge over the line from Porthmadog. Rhoslyn Cottage, on the right, has been occupied on an intermittent basis over the years; although not owned by the railway, its water supply is now taken from a dam in the old Moelwyn Tunnel. *P. Waylett*

Above:
The loop at Dduallt was aligned to avoid the trees which had been planted to beautify the site before World War 2, the new line striking off from the old at the Blaenau end of the Station. On 15 August 1985, in torrential rain, *Blanche* became derailed on the headshunt. The photograph, taken from a Blaenau-bound train, shows the locomotive and observation car together with breakdown van No 999 and *Upnor Castle*; between the van and the Planet was ex-coal wagon No 162 with packing materials. The van, a bogie vehicle obtained from the Navy at Ernesettle and in FR service from 1983, is now a mess vehicle for the Civil Engineering Department. Trains no longer pass at Dduallt and the loop has been converted to a siding with an engineers' run-round loop. *Ray Ruffell*

Tanygrisiau

Above:
When Tanygrisiau, 12 miles from Porthmadog, 1½ from Blaenau Ffestiniog, was demolished it had changed very little from the taking of this photograph in 1887. Only the goods shed now survives, at a point close to the junction between the old and deviation routes. *R. H. Bleasdale*

Right:
The new Tanygrisiau Station was opened on 24 June 1978 and was provided with booking office, tea bar and shop, in the buildings shown, and toilets on the site of the original station buildings, to the left, until the line to Blaenau Ffestiniog was opened four years later. The dam was once considered as part of the formation for the deviation route around the reservoir. The old route followed the line of the road to the power station. On 12 May 1980 *Merddin Emrys* was being prepared to return to Porthmadog after the train had been stranded at Tanygrisiau overnight following a forest fire which affected the railway below Tan-y-bwlch the previous day; at the time the photograph was taken the photographer hadn't appreciated that the proposal that he should act as fireman on the empty stock working was to be taken seriously. A semaphore-signalled passing loop is to be operational here in 1993. *Author*

FESTINIOG Ry. — FESTINIOG Ry
HALF-DAY EXCURSION — HALF-DAY EXCURSION
Return Journey — Outward Journey
1948
Portmadoc — Tanygrisiau
TO — TO
TANYGRISIAU — PORTMADOC
THIRD CLASS — THIRD CLASS
(OVER.)

FESTINIOG RY — FESTINIOG RY
RETURN HALF
Notice. This Ticket is issued subject to the conditions on the Time Tables of the Company — Notice. This Ticket is issued subject to the conditions on the Time Tables of the Company
800
BLAENAU FESTINIOG — Tany Grisiau
TO — TO
TANY GRISIAU — BLAENAU FESTINIOG
First Class 9d — First Class 9d

Revival and Advancement

During the closure much of the track between Boston Lodge and Tan-y-Bwlch had become so overgrown that there was no prospect of running trains throughout immediately. Sand, blown in from the beach, was cleared from the track at Boston Lodge so that a service could be operated across the Cob. The following year, on 23 July 1955, the new management opened for business, carrying 22,000 passengers by the end of the season. The ex-WD Simplex, now named *Mary Ann*, was used at first but *Prince*, fitted with the boiler acquired in 1945, became available at the beginning of August and was used exclusively until 1957.

In 1956 the service was extended to Minffordd, in 1957 to Penrhyn and in 1958 to Tan-y-Bwlch, 7½ miles from Portmadoc. From the 1957 season *Prince* was joined by *Taliesin*, the 1886-built Fairlie.

As the Festiniog revival was getting under way, work was starting on the pumped storage electricity generating scheme at Tanygrisiau. This involved flooding the railway to the north of the Moelwyn Tunnel. The new Company Board made representations in protest, going as far as the House of Lords, but to no avail; railway preservation and restoration was an unknown quantity in the 1950s and it was 1971 before compensation was agreed.

Meanwhile, the railway consolidated its achievements and by 1968, when it was extended a further two miles to Dduallt, it had: returned the other double Fairlie, *Merddin Emrys*, to traffic; acquired Hunslets *Linda* and *Blanche*, and several miles of rail, from the Penrhyn Quarry Railway; been given the American-built *Mountaineer* which had served the World War 1 trenches and, later, a French sugar beet railway; bought Planet diesel *Upnor Castle* from the Welshpool & Llanfair Railway — it had been supplied new to the Navy; put nine bogie and five four-wheel original FR coaches into service; acquired and rebuilt a Lynton & Barnstaple Railway coach, now buffet car No 14, from Devon; rebuilt ex-Welsh Highland Railway carriage No 26, which had been used as a chicken house at Groeslon; and built five new bogie carriages.

Dduallt is one of those rare stations with no road access; from 1968 passengers alighting there could see, for the first time, the results of the efforts to build a new route to Tanygrisiau, work which had commenced in 1965. After a great deal of discussion and negotiation, and fol-lowing several surveys, a route had been chosen which showed that the Festiniog Railway of the 20th century could be as adventurous as that of the 19th. The new line, or deviation, had to gain height to bypass the CEGB's lower reservoir, without introducing any excessive gradients. This condition was met by the construction of a spiral around the hill at Dduallt, the only one on a passenger-carrying railway in the United Kingdom. This work, and much else besides, was carried out by groups of volunteers who came to call themselves 'Deviationists'! The whole project was to take 13 years to bring to fruition, usually with minimal resources.

In addition to the spiral, the new route still required some major civil engineering, including a new (294yd) Moelwyn Tunnel. At the CEGB's insistence the work at the rear of the Tanygrisiau power station, including underground bridges over high-pressure pipelines, had to be carried out by contractor, but the railway was able to use its own labour on the tunnel. Three miners, with experience of Cornish tin and South African diamond mines, were contracted for the job. Construction started in September 1975 and took eight months, although finishing work and track

DIESEL LOCOMOTIVES
Mary Ann
Above right:
The FR's first experience of internal combustion motive power came in 1923, with the acquisition of this ex-War Department Light Railways, 1917-built, 40hp Simplex. It was used to shunt the wharves at Portmadoc and Minffordd and replaced a steam locomotive in performing these duties. *Festiniog Railway Heritage Group Collection*

Right:
The Simplex had neither name nor number but when restoration commenced, and it had become the first operational item of motive power, it became known as *Mary Ann* and was eventually, in 1971, given nameplates to that effect. In 1955 *Mary Ann* hauled the first passenger trains of the new regime. Following the increased availability of steam engines the locomotive was relegated to permanent way duties, for which purpose the 'pagoda' cab was newly fitted when photographed in 1973. Now that less use is made of it, there is a possibility that *Mary Ann* may be returned to its original condition in the 1990s. *FR Co*

POST-REVIVAL LOCOMOTIVES
Linda

Left:
Linda is an 1893 Hunslet 0-4-0ST built for the Penrhyn Quarry Railway. Following a period on loan in 1962, the locomotive was bought by the Festiniog Railway Co the following year, along with sister locomotive *Blanche*. Equipped with an England tender for fuel and additional water, *Linda's* boiler had superheating installed in 1969, became a 2-4-0SST in 1970 (using a wheelset from *Moel Tryfan* for the pony truck) and was converted to oil-firing in 1971. Initially the railway had difficulty in finding a heat resistant black paint which could cope with the additional temperature generated by the oil burning so for a time the locomotive ran with a silver-painted smokebox and chimney. Photographed at Ty Fry, between Minffordd and Penrhyn, on 31 May 1972, the almost invisible exhaust reveals that *Linda* was burning new gas oil, rather than the re-claimed oil adopted as a fuel subsequently. *John Scrace*

Below:
Linda has undergone many changes whilst in Festiniog ownership, including draughting modifications to enable it to burn coal on the gas producer combustion system, as described in the text. During the winter of 1990/91 the locomotive was painted in this lined blue livery and equipped with a removable cab section on the tender. It is shown leaving Porthmadog in this condition on 13 October 1991. *Author*

Blanche

Above:

Blanche, as received from the Penrhyn Quarry Railway, photographed on the tracks approaching the old Boston Lodge engine shed. In 1965 the locomotive received a tender with half-cab and in 1972 was rebuilt as a 2-4-0STT (also using *Moel Tryfan* as the source for the pony truck wheelset) with piston valve cylinders, oil burning and superheating. *Author's Collection*

Below:

The Penrhyn 'Ladies' at Harbour station on 19 April 1986, showing detail differences between the two; the brass star on *Linda's* smokebox door was an affectation by the driver. In 1991/92 *Blanche* is undergoing a major overhaul, which it is anticipated will be completed in time for the locomotives' centenary celebrations in 1993. *Hugh Ballantyne*

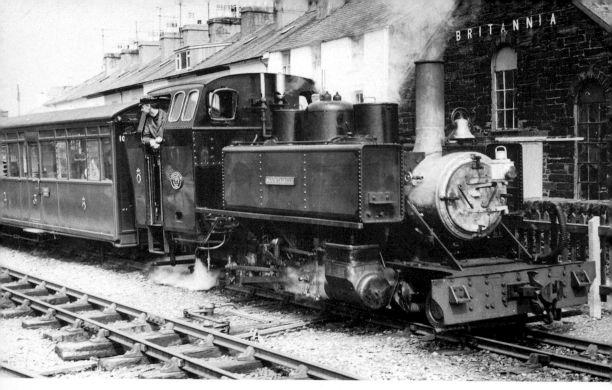

laying meant that it was 1977 before passenger trains passed through.

In that year a temporary station, called Llyn Ystradau and 11½ miles from Porthmadog, was opened alongside the lake to satisfy the conditions attached to the grants received towards the cost of making the tunnel. At the same time outside funding became available to provide labour, in the form of a Manpower Services Commission scheme, for the contractor to build the Power Station section. The Deviationists, meanwhile, had transferred their efforts to the site of the new station at Tanygrisiau, 12 miles from Porthmadog; it was opened on 24 June 1978.

A further four years were to elapse before the FR completed its restoration to Blaenau Ffestiniog. To finish the final 1½ miles it was necessary to build bridges over the Cwmorthin road at Tanygrisiau (at local authority expense — the pre-1974 council had removed it, with permission, when the power station was being built) and the Afon Barlwyd at Glan-y-pwll; to rebuild and raise four footbridges over the line (modern rolling stock is higher than the original); underpin embankments; restore walls and fences; and to establish a site for a terminus.

This work was undertaken by a mixture of volunteers, company staff and job creation labour. Some of the volunteers undertook direct responsibility for particular aspects of the work and were to become specialists in them — bridges, cul-

Mountaineer

Above:

Mountaineer came to the Festiniog Railway in 1967 following an already varied career. Built by the American Locomotive Co (Alco) in 1916, it was shipped over to France for use by the War Department Light Railways. After the war it remained in France and from 1935 was in use on the Tramway de Pithiviers-Toury, serving sugar beet estates. When the tramway closed in 1964 the locomotive was brought to England by an enthusiast who, in 1967, donated it to the FR. Named *Mountaineer* after the first withdrawn England locomotive, the cab was first modified to suit the FR loading gauge and the locomotive went into service. It took the FR a long time to get the measure of *Mountaineer*; as first received steaming was difficult when working hard, due to the internal layout of the boiler; conversion to oil firing in 1971 made a better machine of it. The photograph shows it in that condition, complete with grubby silver-painted smoke box and chimney and bell from the original *Mountaineer. Norman Gurley*

Above right:

Mountaineer's original boiler lasted until the end of 1981, when a new welded boiler, obtained in 1977, was installed, along with piston valves. In 1983 the cab was modified to a more traditional FR design. In this final configuration the locomotive has really proved its worth and on dry rail is capable of handling loads similar to those regularly taken by the Fairlies. The photograph, taken at Boston Lodge in October 1988, shows it in this rebuilt condition; the nameplates were cast from the patterns which existed for the first *Mountaineer. Author*

verts, dry-stone walling, for example. Material and equipment were stored at a depot established at the old engine shed by the level crossing at Glan-y-pwll.

After considering the site of the former LNWR exchange station, opposite the BR Blaenau Ffestiniog station, for a terminus, the FR and BR were persuaded to participate in a local authority scheme to build a new joint station in the town. Funding to clear the site, make the necessary

road alterations for the bridges (which gave the FR access), and for car parks came from several government and non-government bodies, including the European Economic Community. BR inaugurated their part of the new station on 22 March 1982, when the old London & North Western Railway station was closed. The FR followed on 25 May, two days after the 150th anniversary of the Act of Incorporation. The official opening was performed by the Rt Hon

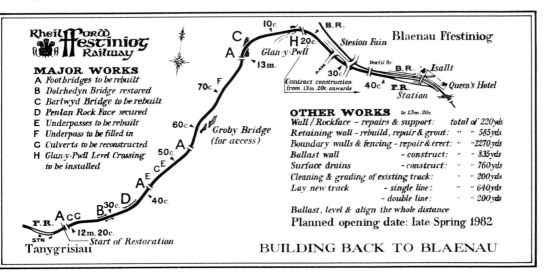

Rheil Fford Festiniog Railway

MAJOR WORKS
A Footbridges to be rebuilt
B Dolrhedyn Bridge restored
C Barlwyd Bridge to be rebuilt
D Penlan Rock Face secured
E Underpasses to be rebuilt
F Underpass to be filled in
G Culverts to be reconstructed
H Glan-y-Pwll Level Crossing to be installed

Blaenau Ffestiniog
Glan-y-Pwll
Stesion Fain
Isallt
Queen's Hotel
F.R. Station
Contract construction from 13m. 20c. onwards

Groby Bridge (for access)

OTHER WORKS to 13m. 20c.
Wall / Rockface – repairs & support: total of 220yds
Retaining wall – rebuild, repair & grout: " " 585yds
Boundary walls & fencing - repair & erect: " " 2270yds
Ballast wall   - construct: " " 835yds
Surface drains   - construct: " " 760yds
Cleaning & grading of existing track: " " 200yds
Lay new track   - single line: " " 640yds
                    - double line: " " 200yds
Ballast, level & align the whole distance
Planned opening date: late Spring 1982

F.R. STN
Tanygrisiau
12m. 20c.
Start of Restoration

BUILDING BACK TO BLAENAU

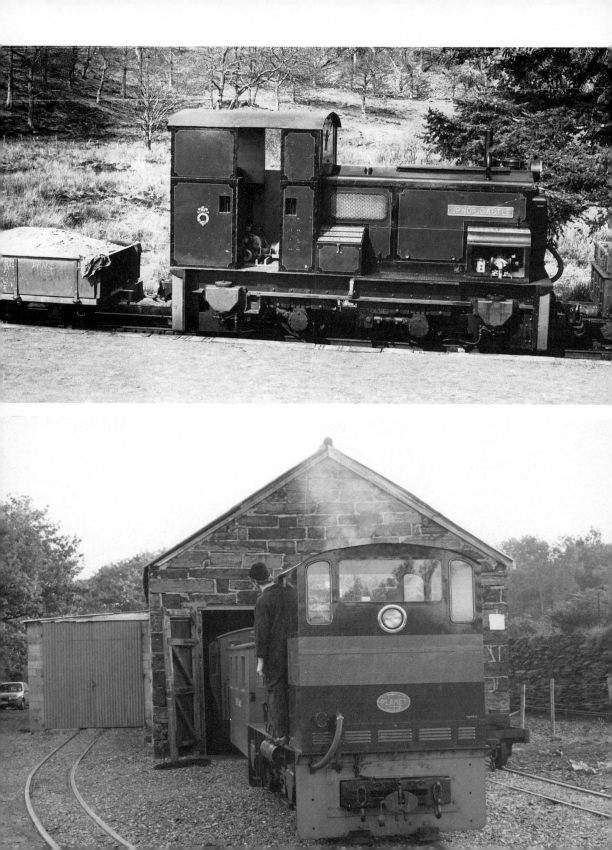

Upnor Castle

Left:
Upnor Castle came to the FR from the Navy, via the Welshpool & Llanfair Light Railway, in 1968. It was built in 1954 by F. C. Hibberd and was transferred to Llanfair Caereinion in 1962. Before it went into service on the FR it was re-gauged from 2ft 6in and the cab was modified to fit the smaller loading gauge. It has been used on both passenger and works trains, as shown here at Dduallt in the 1970s. *Norman Gurley*

Below left:
During its time on the Festiniog *Upnor Castle* has been re-engined twice, in 1971 and 1980, the latest implant being a Gardner 6LXB of 180hp. A fresh paint scheme was applied in July 1990. The photograph shows it shunting carriage stock out of the former Boston Lodge loco shed on 13 October 1991. *Author*

Works trains

Right:
A *Blanche*-hauled works train pulls into Tanygrisiau on 2 May 1981. The train includes *The Lady Diana, Mary Ann*, bogie and four-wheeled Hudson wagons and Vans Nos 1 and 2. It contained materials, including sleepers and ballast, for the reconstruction of the line as far as the Barlwyd Bridge. *Author*

Below:
Harlech Castle propels a works train towards Penrhyn station on 17 August 1991. *Author*

F.R.
LLYN YSTRADAU
DEVIATION
CONSTRUCTION BEGAN
NEAR THIS POINT
ON
JAN. 2, 1965.
G.B. Fox. Engineer.

The Deviation

Left:

In building the deviation line between Dduallt and Tanygrisiau it was necessary to gain height to get around the lakeside. This difference between the routes, looking westwards, is shown on 10 July 1978, 16 days after the deviation line was opened to Tanygrisiau. From Dduallt to a point just off the right of the photograph the new route, about three quarters of a mile, was built totally by volunteers. *R. Fisher*

Below left:

The cutting of the Deviation's first sod is marked by a commemorative stone by the line side, as *Prince* passes with a vintage special on 13 October 1991. The train consists of van No 2, 'Bug Box' No 5, van No 10, No 16 and No 12. *Author*

Below:

As the train runs alongside Llyn Ystradau the old route is often visible on the lake bed, which can be seen to the left of *Earl of Merioneth* on 19 August 1989. For a few months in 1977 trains ran to a temporary terminus, called Llyn Ystradau, near this spot. Immediately behind the locomotive are open tourist cars Nos 37/8, built in 1971 on Hudson bogie wagon underframes. *Author*

George Thomas MP, then speaker of the House of Commons, now Lord Tonypandy, on 30 April 1983.

Whilst great efforts were being made to regain the Blaenau terminus, many changes had also taken place on the operating railway. The Harbour Station headquarters had been extended to give larger sales, catering and office space.

Boston Lodge Works had a new erecting shop and metal-working facilities, enabling the building of a new double Fairlie, *Earl of Merioneth*, which emerged in 1979, and six steel-bodied coaches. From 1970 the locomotives were converted to burn oil, eliminating the fire risk in the woodland which had developed alongside the route during the closure. Also, at Boston Lodge, the facilities provided in a new carriage shop resulted in an improvement in the condition of the timber-bodied coaches. The former exchange yard at Minffordd was developed as a permanent way depot and road/rail interchange. A volunteers' hostel was also provided here, following the successful conversion of the Penrhyn station buildings for the same purpose.

Between 1978 and 1982 the inclusive tours to Llyn Stwlan (the upper lake of the CEGB pumped storage scheme) and the slate caverns were operated via Tanygrisiau, buses completing the link. From 1982 the Blaenau interchange was marketed with BR as the 'Festiniog Link' and encouraged the promotion of both circular tours and excursions using the Cambrian Coast and the Conwy Valley lines as well as the FR — just as Hughes reported on in 1890. In 1982 the Llyn Stwlan tour was replaced by a Portmeirion connection, otherwise these arrangements still stand. The existence of the link enabled BR to extend its Red Star parcels service to Porthmadog and stations to Pwllheli, making the FR then the only private railway to offer a through parcels service, a facility which came into its own only when the National Eisteddfod was held in Porthmadog in 1987.

Earl of Merioneth

Below:
The 'new' *Earl of Merioneth* was built around the boiler acquired for the 'old' *Earl* and using that locomotive's power bogies. It was completed in 1979, coinciding with *Merddin Emrys's* centenary. The new locomotive was quite an ugly brute but the railway's resources were being concentrated on the push to Blaenau at the time it was built; locomotive aesthetics did not come very high on the company's list of priorities. *Earl of Merioneth* did take advantage of the technical advances available and had sufficient capacity for running to Blaenau without taking water en route. It was launched on an unsuspecting world on 23 June 1979, on which occasion this photograph was taken. *Author*

Bottom:
In 1988 *Earl of Merioneth* was taken into the workshops for an intermediate overhaul and it was decided to soften its appearance and apply a revised livery at the same time. By the time it returned to traffic in September 1989 its power bogies had received sufficient attention to make them better than new. It is expected that further changes to the *Earl's* appearance will be made during the major overhaul due to commence after the completion of the new double-engine superstructure. The photograph shows the locomotive being made ready for service on 16 August 1991. *Author*

1986 was an eventful year which saw the railway celebrate its 150th anniversary. *Prince* went into traffic in the red livery of the 1900s and helped launch the Conwy Valley and Cambrian Coast Sprinters; a gala weekend was held, with many attractions laid on for an appreciative audience; a 7½in-gauge railway operated at Tan-y-bwlch; de Winton vertical boilered locomotive *Chaloner*, ex-Pen-yr-orsedd slate quarry, visited from Leighton Buzzard; BR Class 47 locomotive No 47645 was named *Robert F. Fairlie Locomotive Engineer 1831-1885* at Blaenau Ffestiniog; another ex-Navy Planet diesel was restored for use on passenger trains and named *Conway Castle*; *Mountaineer* visited the Vale of Rheidol Railway; the privately owned *Britomart*, also ex-Pen-yr-orsedd and based at Boston Lodge, visited the Leighton Buzzard Railway and a train of restored slate wagons was operated from Blaenau Ffestiniog by gravity.

The return to Blaenau was achieved only at the expense of a large overdraft and further development was hampered by the need to service it. Solutions considered to improve the railway's capital base were in turn hampered by the Victorian statutes which governed it. Eventually a scheme was devised which calculated that there was a certain amount of prestige to be gained by issuing stock which had been authorised by Parliament in the last century, taking advantage of a small amount of unissued stock. The Company offered £1 shares with the proviso that each application for one share be accompanied by another for a £250 4% debenture, requiring a minimum £251 investment. Certificates were designed in a Victorian style and a lavish prospectus was printed. Launched in October 1987, over £½ million was raised.

In 1988 the Railway commemorated the 125th anniversary of steam traction with another gala; the highlights of this were the operation of the Welsh Highland Railway's 2-6-2T *Russell*; the return to traffic of *Merddin Emrys*, newly overhauled and resplendent in Victorian outline and livery; and the operation of a mixed train in the traditional manner.

The railway's finances weren't the only aspect requiring attention after 1982, for many parts of the railway looked decidedly run down. The Parks & Gardens Department was established and a start was made to 'de-tattyfy' the line. Activities including clearance, planting, painting and refurbishing of buildings now regularly attract parties of over 100 volunteers, including paid staff off duty, the very young, the less young and

Britomart

Below:
Britomart is one of what is becoming an increasing number of privately owned locomotives based on the FR. Built by Hunslet for the Pen-yr-orsedd Quarry in 1899, it came to the railway in 1966. It is usually steamed for the benefit of its owners and is sometimes used for the benefit of the host railway, hence visits to the Leighton Buzzard Railway, the Bala Lake Railway and the Welsh Highland Railway. It is seen approaching Minffordd on 25 April 1987, when it ran two trips to Rhiw Goch in connection with the FR Society's AGM, held that day. The coach behind Britomart, No 23, is a 56-seat third class car built for the North Wales Narrow Gauge Railways by the Ashbury Carriage & Wagon Co in 1894; it was transferred to the FR by the Welsh Highland Railway in 1936, in exchange for three bogie wagons. The brake vehicle is No 11, built in 1880 as a bogie brake van and converted to a brake/saloon/observation car in 1957/58. *Author*

many who are new to volunteering. All this voluntary effort has been supported by the company, which, for its part, erected a platform canopy at Porthmadog and instituted a new regime for carriage painting, whereby the whole fleet can be repainted every three years; a new, brighter, two-colour carriage livery was also introduced. On the operating side, in 1987 an automated train crossing was introduced at Tan-y-bwlch, followed two years later by a similar installation at Minffordd.

Attention has also been paid to the railway's heritage with the creation of an improved museum in the Porthmadog Goods Shed, the turning out of *Prince*, *Merddin Emrys* and several carriages in historic liveries. The operation of gravity and mixed trains comes into the Festiniog Railway Heritage Group's sphere of influence and has encouraged volunteers to restore several wagons and vans for use on special occasions. The last item of un-restored carriage stock, van No 10, which was used in the early years of the railway's revival and then put to one side, was restored for use with the Vintage Train in 1991. Also in 1991 four-wheel car No 7, the open Brown, Marshalls & Co vehicle of 1863 was made available for special occasions, as was the unique hearse van. The latter ran for the first time in preservation, for funeral purposes, on 26 October 1991.

Above:
Further framework modification was carried out to *Prince* during the 1988 overhaul, as seen in this photograph taken at Minffordd during the gala commemorating the FR's 125th anniversary of the use of steam traction — 'FR Steam 125'. Oil-firing equipment was fitted to the locomotive during the overhaul completed in 1980. The old livery was restored for the Railway's 150th anniversary in 1986. *Author*

Conway Castle
Above right:
In the 1980s the railway required a second diesel suitable for passenger use and bought another Hibberd-built machine, this time from RNAD Ernesettle, in 1982; it is four years younger than *Upnor Castle*. Following re-gauging and re-engining, also with a Gardner 6LXB, a new superstructure was fitted before the locomotive entered service in 1986. It was named *Conway Castle*, in both Welsh and English, by the Mayor of Conwy on 5 July 1986. *Norman Gurley*

Right:
At first in FR service *Conway Castle* was painted a striking orange and black livery. When it was decided to develop a new livery for the push-pull set *Conway Castle* was repainted to match in 1990, following the installation of the electronics for remote operation when working in push-pull mode. On this locomotive the Gresham & Craven twin pipe, quick release, vacuum brake is the same as that used on BR first generation DMUs. Photographed on 9 March 1991. *Author*

The close of the 1980s brought further opportunities for development with the aid of outside funding. Known as InCa, for the scheme was to INcrease CApacity, the following were funded: three new carriages equipped with heating and public address, for the Push-Pull train; a 10-car carriage shed with maintenance facilities at Boston Lodge; a boiler and superstructure for a new double Fairlie of traditional outline, allowing the *Earl of Merioneth*'s superstructure to be withdrawn for overhaul; a spare Fairlie power bogie; improvements to the buffet/bar at Harbour Station; new toilets and improved café facilities at Tan-y-bwlch; permanent platform buildings with canopy and a carriage siding at Blaenau Ffestiniog; and a new diesel locomotive for exclusive use of the permanent way department.

Harlech Castle
Above left:
In 1985 the FR received a new six-wheel diesel locomotive on loan for demonstration purposes. No 3767 was one of six built by Baguley-Drewry in 1983 for a cancelled export order to Mozambique; the builders had subsequently ceased trading and the liquidator was looking for buyers. Despite being too big for the FR's loading gauge, the loco was used on works trains before being returned in 1986. It is shown in Minffordd yard, with *Moel Hebog* behind, on 22 August 1985. *Author*

Centre left:
When the InCa scheme was being developed in 1989 it was decided to fund a Civil Engineering Department locomotive, to take the strain off the smaller diesel locomotives. Contact was made with No 3767's new owners and it was part-exchanged for the ex-Harrogate Gas Works Peckett which the FR had owned since 1955 but never used. On returning to Wales the locomotive was modified to suit the FR's requirements at the Porthmadog works of Winson Engineering. On 24 April 1991 No 3767 was officially named, in English and Welsh, *Harlech Castle*, at Blaenau Ffestiniog by the Secretary of State for Wales, Rt Hon David Hunt MP and his daughter, Daisy. The photograph was taken at Boston Lodge in September 1990. *Author*

Moel Hebog
Left:
Moel Hebog was a Hunslet mines loco built in 1955. It came to the FR from Shaw Colliery, Yorkshire, in 1969 and was first used following the fitting of a cab, obtained from the Talyllyn Railway, in 1975. Vacuum brakes were fitted at the same time and the locomotive featured in the Railway's first experiment with push-pull working. The photograph shows *Moel Hebog* with quarrymen's coach No 8, built at Boston Lodge in 1885/86, and a bogie oil tank wagon on the Mineral line at Minffordd on 19 October 1984. *Author*

L&NWR Exchange

Below:
The FR's interchange station with the L&NWR was opened in 1881. The double track was actually two independent lines — mineral and passenger - an arrangement discussed by Spring in his report. The view is towards Glan-y-pwll. *Commercial postcard — North Wales Post Card Co*

Bottom:
From 1923 track layouts in Blaenau were changed and the dedicated mineral line done away with. A loop remained at Glan-y-pwll crossing and another was installed at the station in 1930. *Merddin Emrys* arrives on 23 August 1937 and the top shunter waits in the Glan-y-pwll loop to remove slate empties for the Oakeley and Llechwedd quarries. *R. E. Tustin*

NARROW & BROAD GUAGE STATIONS, & SLATE QUARRIES, BLAENAU FESTINIOG.

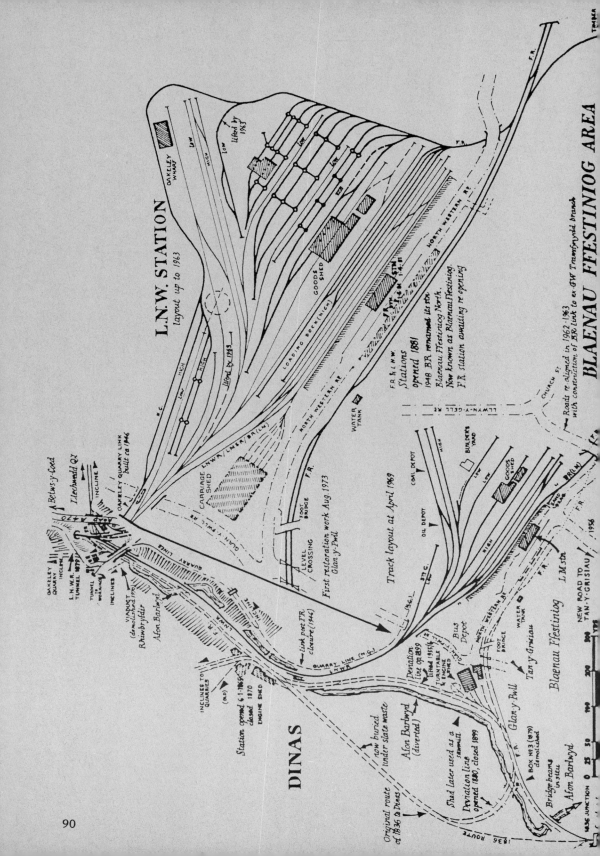

BLAENAU FFESTINIOG AREA

L.N.W. STATION
Layout up to 1963

DINAS

Track layout at April 1969

First restoration work Aug. 1973
Glan-y-Pwll

Blaenau Ffestiniog

F.R. & L.N.W.
Stations
opened 1881
1948 BR renamed its stn
Blaenau Ffestiniog North.
Now known as Blaenau Ffestiniog.
F.R. station awaiting re opening

Roads re aligned in 1962-1963
with construction of BR link to ex GW Trawsfynydd branch

90

Right:

In March 1955 a Simplex-hauled train made its way up to Blaenau Ffestiniog to recover materials; it is seen passing through the L&NWR Exchange station on the return. The canopy remains in use at the Manod football ground and the water tank plinth remained until the Glan-y-don slate tip was removed to the ground on the right in the 1970s. The footbridge visible behind the train marks the approximate location of the present A496 road crossing of the Railway.
Geoff Charles

Below:

Linda approaches Glan-y-pwll level crossing on 17 August 1989, passing the site of the former L&NWR Exchange station; the original FR line into Blaenau Ffestiniog had followed the road in the foreground, that to the right only being built to aid the power station construction and that beyond the junction being re-aligned at least twice. By this time the British Rail station across the road had been closed for over seven years. *Author*

GWR Exchange

Left:
The Great Western Railway Exchange platform at Blaenau Ffestiniog, opened in 1883, marks the location of the former narrow gauge Ffestiniog & Blaenau Railway terminus. On the original 1887 print a Fairlie standing in Duffws station is discernible under the bridge. In 1992 most of the area shown here is a car park, with the BR line to Trawsfynydd cutting across the centre and the FR over on the right. *R. H. Bleasdale*

Below left:
The approach to Duffws was controlled from the No 1 signal box, left rear, which was removed in 1929. The trident signal opposite then being transferred to the Cob at the same time. The quarrymen's train is stabled on the left, suggesting that the photograph may have been taken during the period that FR passenger trains terminated at the GWR platform in the 1920s.
Adrian Gray Collection

Below:
By March 1955 the FR side of the GWR station already showed signs of the vandalism which was to occur as the site became less used. Until 1962 the line shown remained in use by Maenoffern and Votty quarries which were still passing slate to the former L&NWR trans-shipment yard. With the Central Station development in 1982 the railways swapped sides. The telegraph pole by the widened formation on the left indicates the location of the former (1879-1912) FR siding to the Newborough Slate Mill; the formation at this location is now occupied by the water tower.
G. E. Baddeley

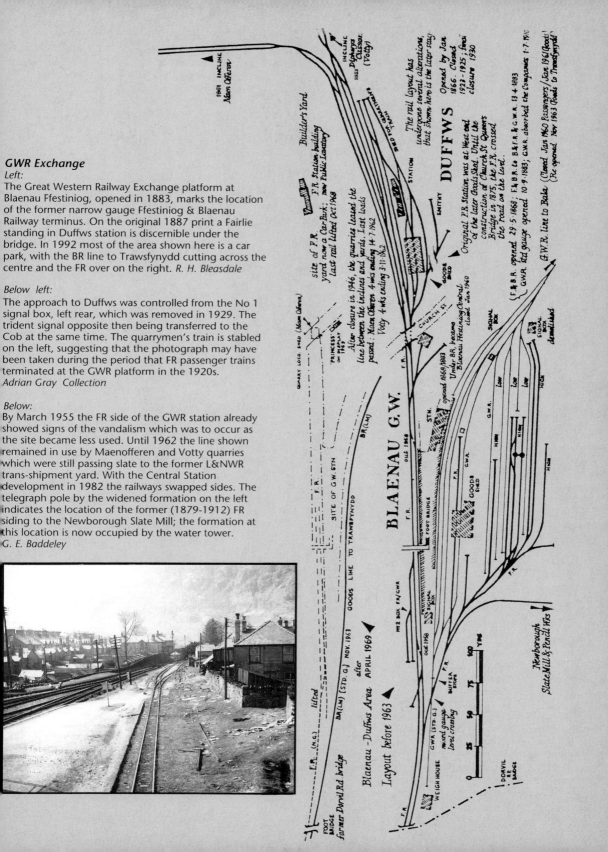

Blaenau - Duffws Area
Layout before 1963

BLAENAU G.W.

DUFFWS

The rail layout has undergone several alterations, that shown here is the later stage.

Opened by Jan. 1866. Closed 1922 - 1925 ; final closure 1930

Original F.R. station was at West end of the later Goods Shed. Until the construction of Church St Queens Bridge in 1875, the F.R. crossed the road on the level.

(F.& B.R. opened 29.5.1868 ; F.& B.R. to B.& F.R. & G.W.R. 13.4.1883
G.W.R. std gauge opened 10.9.1883 ; G.W.R. absorbed the Companies 1.7.1883)

G.W.R. line to Bala (Closed Jan 1960 Passengers/Jan 1961(Goods)
(Re-opened Nov 1963 Goods to Trawsfynydd)

Newborough Slate Mill & Pencil Wks

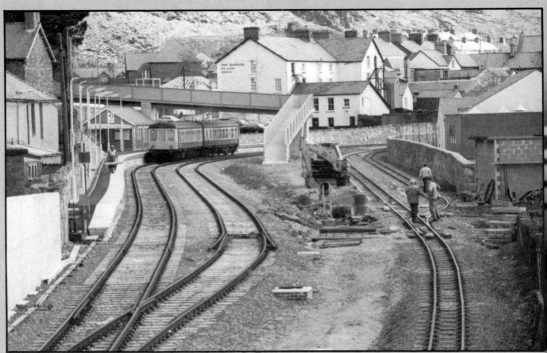

Steam Locomotive Developments

No new locomotives were constructed during the railway's decline and the decline also explains why none received the advances in steam technology being incorporated elsewhere. It was for the preservationists to bring in these improvements.

Had the slate business remained buoyant, improvements to power and efficiency, such as superheating, might well have been introduced at that time. The major benefit of superheating is that condensation of steam in the cylinders can be reduced or eliminated. Condensation is undesirable because of the loss of volume and pressure and thus loss of power and efficiency. Superheating, therefore, yields economies in fuel and water consumption but the increased temperature and dryness puts much greater demands on the locomotive's lubrication. This, coupled with the added complexity of the boiler construction, slowed its adoption. The lubrication was particularly troublesome with slide valve operation, and the use of superheating was usually accompanied by a change to piston valves which have other advantages, such as reduced wire drawing.

The Fairlie engines have a neat but cramped arrangement of valve gear inside the closely spaced bogie frames; and even on the new locomotive now being built with superheat the railway is adhering to slide valves because of lack of space.

The rebuilding of the railway by volunteers captured the public's imagination, and passenger traffic in the 1960s grew rapidly. Even with the acquisition of three steam locomotives from other sources, all the engines at that time were simple saturated machines with slide valves. To keep pace with heavier loads, the opportunity was taken, when reboiling, to introduce superheating using a Melesco design of header and two five inch diameter flues with two 1½ inch diameter elements per flue. This, of course, was repeated in both barrels of the Fairlie locomotives. Superheating produced an increase in steam temperature of about 20°F over the saturated steam temperature of 371°F at 160 psi boiler pressure. This modest temperature rise improved performance significantly and the change was accompanied by major lubrication

David Lloyd George

Right:
In 1989 the FR had the chance of some development funding so, having discovered structural weaknesses in the Hunslet double-engine boilers (probably not unrelated to their being 2ft longer than their predecessors), it was decided to finance a new double-engine superstructure. It is expected that this will allow two double-engines to be kept in traffic, whilst the third receives an overhaul. The existence of a spare power bogie (construction financed from the same source) and an identical power bogie being built for the *Taliesin* replica allows all sorts of exciting permutations to be conjured up! The photograph shows one of the boiler barrels and firebox plates, including one of the throat plates lying horizontally on the bench, at the works of Bloomfield Steel Construction in the West Midlands, on 8 March 1991. *Author*

Right:
Construction of the new boiler was approaching completion when the firebox was photographed on 23 April 1991. The openings for the fire hole doors can be seen indicated; at this stage the inner firebox had not been installed. The boiler was delivered to Minffordd on 1 August 1991 and completion of the superstructure is proposed for June 1992. It is intended that it be named *David Lloyd George*; the famous politician used the FR when he was a practising solicitor in Portmadoc. *Author*

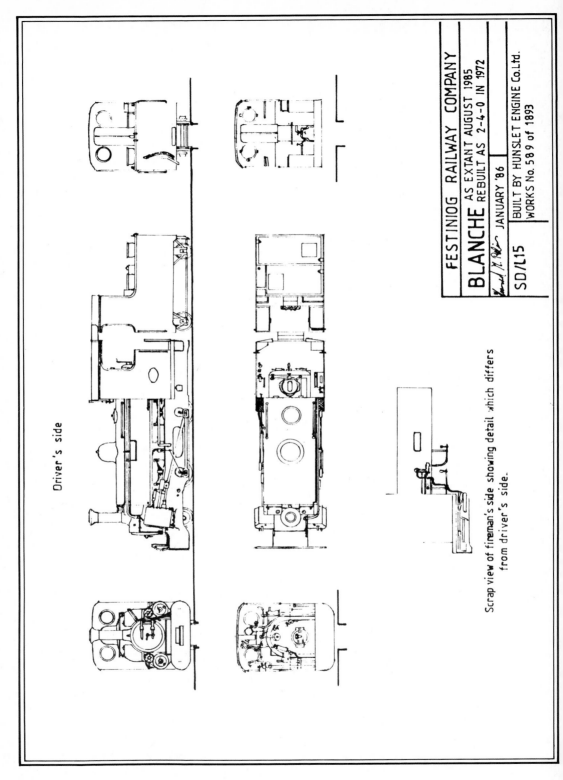

Driver's side

FESTINIOG RAILWAY COMPANY

BLANCHE AS EXTANT AUGUST 1985
REBUILT AS 2-4-0 IN 1972

JANUARY '86

SD/L15

BUILT BY HUNSLET ENGINE Co.Ltd.
WORKS No. 58 9 of 1893

Scrap view of fireman's side showing detail which differs from driver's side.

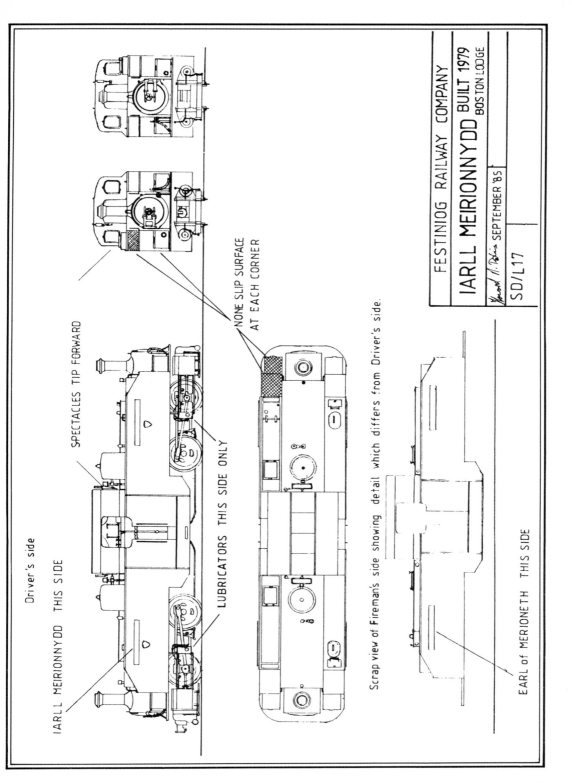

Driver's side

IARLL MEIRIONNYDD THIS SIDE

SPECTACLES TIP FORWARD

LUBRICATORS THIS SIDE ONLY

NONE SLIP SURFACE
AT EACH CORNER

Scrap view of Fireman's side showing detail which differs from Driver's side.

EARL of MERIONETH THIS SIDE

FESTINIOG RAILWAY COMPANY

IARLL MEIRIONNYDD BUILT 1979
BOSTON LODGE

SEPTEMBER '85

SD/L17

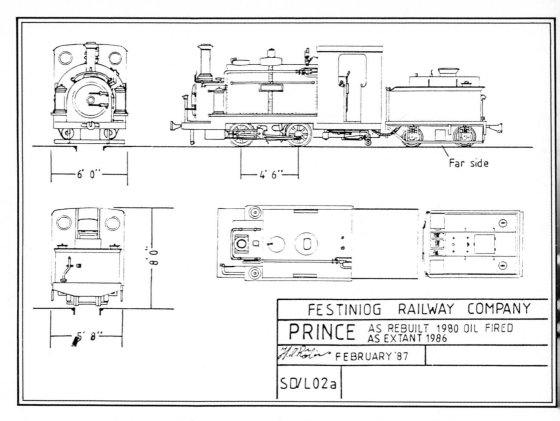

FESTINIOG RAILWAY COMPANY

PRINCE AS REBUILT 1980 OIL FIRED
AS EXTANT 1986

FEBRUARY '87

SD/L02a

Far side

6' 0"   4' 6"   8' 0"   5' 8"

improvements. Mechanical lubrication pumps were fitted with boiler pressure atomisation and applied to key areas. Later, superheaters were fitted with an FR design of divided header with the elements welded into position, which has the advantage that the header/element assembly could be hydraulically tested on the bench.

With the locomotives being converted to oil firing problems then arose with elements corroding and cracking, particularly on the return bends. After much experimenting, the solution found and adopted is to use 316 grade stainless steel bends; after eight years the railway has had no failures of bends.

In 1982 an improved design substantially increased the superheat to 70°F above saturation temperature without lubrication or other associated problems. The boiler for the new Double Fairlie locomotive will utilise a further improved design with separate headers, for wet and dry steam, and four flues, eight elements per boiler barrel.

By 1972/73 all locomotives were converted to oil firing. Boiler pressures were raised when boilers were replaced, superheat introduced and the performance achieved was well above designers' intentions. The spur to this endeavour to improve

efficiency was the cost of fuel, one of the biggest items in the accounts.

It is not surprising that the Festiniog Railway's logo features the unique double engine. It was the forerunner to the vast range of Garratts used throughout the world and, fittingly, the railway owns the first of this great line of engines, on loan to the National Railway Museum at York, although it is too large for our own loading gauge. The preservation of our heritage encourages the use of these powerful locomotives and considerable attention has been given to improving them to maximise efficiency but the railway has also gone to great pains to understand the thinking behind the original design.

The original Fairlies had what is known as a 'wagon top' boiler with a characteristic conical shape sloping down from the dome towards the smokebox (at each end). The new locomotive, currently under construction, should be indistinguishable from the original to the outside observer. The boiler is of all-welded construction to current BS2790, but it represents a return to 19th century design thinking in regard to the use of the boiler as a structural element of the locomotive as a whole. This is achieved by using a conical section in each barrel giving a larger

In 1986/87 *Merddin Emrys* underwent a sponsored
overhaul which had a major impact on its appearance,
the most noticeable aspect of which was the recreation
of its Victorian livery. Other cosmetic details were the
fake rivet heads (rubber initially, then metal) affixed to
the tanks and the fitting of new painted domes. New
power bogies, built at Boston Lodge, were fitted at the
same time. The locomotive is seen standing on an
inspection pit at Boston Lodge during disposal on 23
October 1988. *Author*

diameter in way of the fireboxes. This gives more
strength to cope with vertical track forces and
the out-of-balance vertical wheel forces arising
from partial wheel balancing of the reciprocating
parts. The original 'wagon top' design did not
employ truly conical barrel sections but a raised
upper section only, with flat sides requiring the
use of internal horizontal tension stays to support
the flat sides against boiler pressure. These stays
seem to have been very troublesome in service,
hence the adoption of the new conical design.

Track forces and thermal stresses have given
the railway trouble with cracking in the throat
plates, ie where the barrel joins the firebox, on
the present double engines, which use neither

the original 'wagon top' design nor the new conical design but a conventional cylindrical barrel. It
is to be hoped that the new arrangement will
have got it right.

Currently under construction in the workshops
are two new Fairlie power bogies. When completed, the railway will have six power bogies,
three double engine boilers, three superstructures
and tanks and one single Fairlie locomotive boiler
and superstructure. This will allow enormous flex-
ibility because all power bogies are interchangeable and can be replaced in a day under any of
these engines. This is a special virtue because, at
peak times, the workshop staff is depleted
because of driving duties.

Despite improvements, the steam locomotive
as a means of motive power is relatively ineffi-
cient, burning some three gallons per mile compared with about four miles to the gallon for a
diesel locomotive. Maintenance of steam engines
is also far greater.

As already mentioned, fuel cost is a major item.
The railway's fuel policy is presently to remain
with waste oils donated or purchased. This suits
the railway because volunteers visit garages and
depots and get free (used) oil. The FR uses about
55,000 gallons per annum at a cost of about

£35,000. The viscosity of waste oils varies from 28 to over 3,000sec. The waste is mixed with proprietary oils to get a uniform viscosity of about 120sec (which matches the burner settings) and centrifuge to get rid of solids. The most economical ratio of waste to proprietary oil is about 3-1 but this requires more waste oil than our volunteers are successful in obtaining. In the early 1980s fuel costs were typically £50,000 per annum. This was the incentive for a lot of research and in-service flue gas analysis to improve combustion. Also a great deal of work was done on the alternative of the coal-fired gas-producer combustion system.

This system gasifies cheap grade soft coal, instead of burning it on the grate. It burns the gas produced in secondary air admitted over the firebed. Air flow through the grate is limited to about 30% of that required normally, thus eliminating the damaging effect of air flow on the firebed. Steam is introduced into the primary air, which reacts chemically with the coal and cools the firebed to below the clinker-forming temperature, allowing a thick firebed to be maintained.

Above:
From 1961 *Livingston Thompson* was renamed again, this time carrying the name *Earl of Merioneth*, one of the Duke of Edinburgh's titles, bilingually. Withdrawn in 1971, initially for installation of a new parallel Hunslet boiler, the superstructure was set aside for preservation. In 1988 it regained its power bogies and it was restored cosmetically to 1910 period appearance. Becoming *Livingston Thompson* again, it has been placed on loan to the National Railway Museum, York, following a handing over ceremony at Tan-y-bwlch on 16 October 1988, the occasion of the photograph — *Livingston Thompson* was towed thence by *Merddin Emrys*. In 1989 the locomotive was displayed at York and in 1990 at Swindon, as part of the 'National Railway Museum on Tour' display in the former Great Western Railway workshops. *Author*

Above right:
The new (1973) erecting shop on 9 March 1991. The picture shows: (foreground) the boiler cradle for the InCa-funded Fairlie; (centre) two power bogies, under construction, inverted, one as a spare for the double-engines, one for the 'Taliesin 2000' project; (rear) the sheet metal folding equipment, used when building the bodies of the steel bodied-carriages. *Author*

The chemical reaction increases the calorific value of the combustion gas. The secondary air inlets are placed to give optimum coal particle separation and good mixing of gas and air.

Gas-producer combustion allows hard working for long periods without fire cleaning, due to the absence of clinker. The almost complete combustion means good fuel efficiency, clean tubes and, therefore, good heat transference within the boiler.

The technology is available to the railway should the relative fuel oil to coal price ratio rise again. Once the conversion has been done changing from one to the other is not too difficult.

Finally, there is an exciting scheme underway to provide the Festiniog Railway with another new locomotive by the year 2000. Called 'Taliesin 2000', the scheme will fund the building of a new 0-4-4T single Fairlie after the style of the original *Taliesin*; for many the single Fairlie, a feature of the North Wales Narrow Gauge Railways and the Welsh Highland Railway as well as the FR, is a vital part of the line's heritage and something which should be restored. Over 220 people will pay £60 a year for 12 years in support of their beliefs. By December 1991 over £50,000 had been raised and construction of the power bogie was well in hand. Since the project started several parts from the original locomotive have been identified, around Boston Lodge, which will be incorporated into the new locomotive.

(Based on a paper presented by David Pollock, General Manager 1983-1991, to the Institution of Mechanical Engineers on 5 November 1991.)

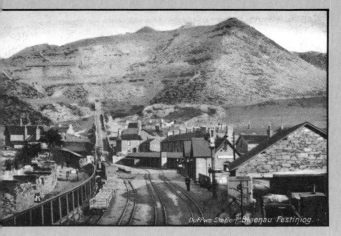

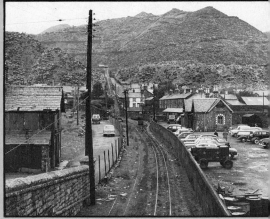

Duffws

Above:
Duffws station was opened in 1866 and finally closed in 1931, although it had also been closed in 1923/24. It was 13 miles from Portmadoc and 720ft above sea level. From the right this picture, taken in c1900, shows the goods shed, the station building, locomotive water tank, quarrymen's train shelter, and the incline to Votty (straight on); the line to Maenofferen turned off to the left at the foot of the Votty line. *Commercial postcard — The Wrench Series*

Above:
Following the withdrawal of passenger services from Duffws the non-operational land reverted to the land owner, to whom rents were still owing, and, fenced off from the railway, was converted to a car park by the local authority. The 1870s station building became, and remains, public conveniences. This 1950s photograph shows part of the quarrymen's train shelter still existing at that time. *Author's Collection*

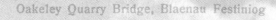

Oakeley Quarry Bridge, Blaenau Festiniog

Dinas

Below left:

Dinas was the original upper terminus of the Festiniog Railway, remaining so until 1870. The line beyond the station served the Oakeley (left) and Llechwedd (straight on) quarries. The viaduct, demolished in 1970, had been modified by the L&NWR when the standard gauge line from Betws-y-coed, behind the wall on the right, was built in 1879 and connected the Oakeley Quarry to its Glan-y-don tip. The photographer has captured the track gang at work c1910. *Commercial postcard — The Glorian Series*

Boston Lodge Halt

Right:

Mountaineer at Boston Lodge Halt in August 1982. This halt is provided with a short platform but has no form of passenger shelter. The former locomotive shed is obscured by the trees on the right. Behind the photographer stands a garage which used the former Boston Lodge turntable as a foundation. *Author*

Plas Halt

Below:

Plas Halt is the smallest public station on the FR. Opened in 1963 it serves the Snowdonia National Park Study Centre at Plas Tan-y-bwlch. A team of volunteers was responsible for the stone-built shelter there which was finished in the 1980s. The same group has started on a larger structure, which will include toilet facilities, at Dduallt. *Author*

Passenger Coach Developments

With some 30 coaches, maintenance, especially on some of the historic vehicles, can be costly. The older bogie vehicles have heavy wrought-iron frames and a poor load-to-tare weight ratio. A large capital programme, known as the 'InCa' (INcreased CApacity) Programme, will allow the railway to be more selective in the use of these older vehicles. They do, however, come into their own on a special 'heritage' train run at weekends in the summer months, wholly manned by volunteers and hauled by *Prince*, and a joy to the enthusiasts.

Three new coaches are nearing completion under this 'InCa' programme. They are a distinct step forward in design and technology, offering

POST-PRESERVATION CARRIAGES
Wooden-bodied stock
Right:
From 1964 the FR started building new passenger stock, constructing wooden bodies on steel frames. The first was No 24, which became No 104 after a new series for this stock was started at No 100 to commemorate the passenger centenary in 1965. By 1970, six cars had been built in this series; they were higher than any previous FR stock except No 14 (the former Lynton & Barnstaple Railway buffet car which had entered FR service in 1963) and all had corridor connections. The underframes and bogies were built at Boston Lodge and the body sections were fabricated in Birkenhead. Three of the cars were nominally identical, having two third class saloons seating 32 and a first class centre-corridor compartment, except that No 105 also had a toilet compartment. The first, now No 104, was subject to major body renewal in 1985, when the centre corridor first class compartment became a side corridor compartment and the window frames were all replaced. *Author*

Right:
Two other cars in the 'Centenary' series are also similar, in that Nos 100 and 101 both had guards' compartments, with a first class observation saloons and a first class buffet saloon. The buffet saloon have Pullman armchairs, as do the first class compartments in Nos 104/6. The sixth vehicle, No 103, is a buffet car with a large kitchen, whose use has recently been called into question due to recent legislation regarding food preparation. The photograph was taken at Boston Lodge Halt on 25 April 1987, when the two colour livery was fairly new. The electrical connection adjacent to the vacuum pipe is for charging car batteries at Porthmadog. The third vehicle in is No 103. Nos 100-6 are known as 'Barns', due to their similarity in profile to No 14. *Author*

improved comfort. The vehicles are aluminium on steel underframes with self-steering bogies. A light framework is clad in single 30ft sheets of aluminium, epoxy glued to the frame and carefully insulated from the steel underframe to avoid corrosion. The sides and ceilings inside are lined with carpet texture materials, floors are carpeted and seats soft furnished. Heating, formerly not available on the FR, is provided by a propane gas boiler and continuous skirting board water radiators, which are unobtrusive. Good fluorescent lighting and public address facility complete this thumbnail sketch. These three coaches are push-pull fitted with the two-pipe vacuum brake and driver control wires so that, with the other three push-pull vehicles, we have the capacity of running up to six cars in this way, giving a high passenger/train crew ratio. The new coaches are not only well insulated, both in sound and heat, but the new bogies are much quieter and give a

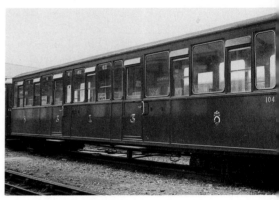

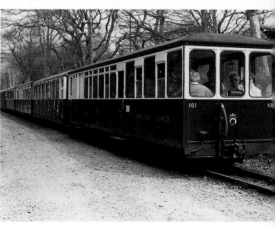

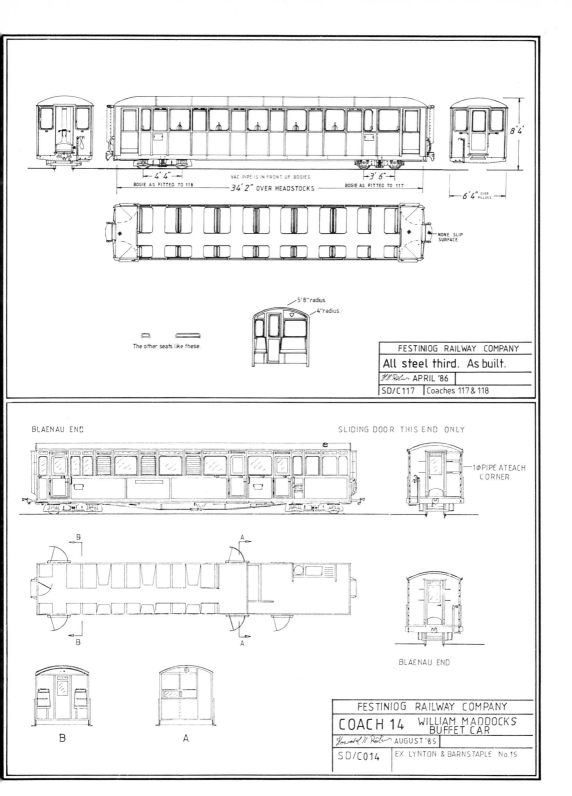

VAC PIPE IS IN FRONT OF BOGIES

4'4"
BOGIE AS FITTED TO 118

34'2" OVER HEADSTOCKS

3'6"
BOGIE AS FITTED TO 117

8'4'

6'4" OVER PILLARS

NONE SLIP SURFACE

The other seats like these.

5'8" radius.

4" radius.

FESTINIOG RAILWAY COMPANY

All steel third. As built.

APRIL '86

SD/C117 | Coaches 117 & 118

BLAENAU END

SLIDING DOOR THIS END ONLY

1 Ø PIPE AT EACH CORNER

B

A

B

A

BLAENAU END

B

A

FESTINIOG RAILWAY COMPANY

COACH 14   WILLIAM MADDOCKS BUFFET CAR

AUGUST '85

SD/C014 | EX. LYNTON & BARNSTAPLE No.15

Steel bodied stock

Above:

A further series of six coaches, Nos 117-21, was built at Boston Lodge between 1977 and 1981. They are third class saloons with steel bodies built on underframes obtained from the Isle of Man Railway. The seating was adapted from that acquired from scrapped buses — despite its source it did then provide the best third class seating on the railway. Nos 119 and 120 have toilet compartments; the latter, in traffic from 1980, was photographed on 25 April 1987. In 1990 lower body panel corrosion was cut out of No 120, the remainder treated and covered with aluminium panels to give a flush finish, matching the push-pull set. *Author*

Below:

It was found that the opening windows fitted to this series were subject to failure and maintenance was awkward, requiring internal body panel removal, so the last in the series, No 121, was given a simpler pattern, as seen here; even the vertical sliding window retained in the door will not stay closed whilst the vehicle is parked. Removing the vertical sliding windows also eliminated a potential access for rainwater to the inner body panels. No 121 has been modified to run in the push-pull set and now has gas powered central heating and new seating. *Author*

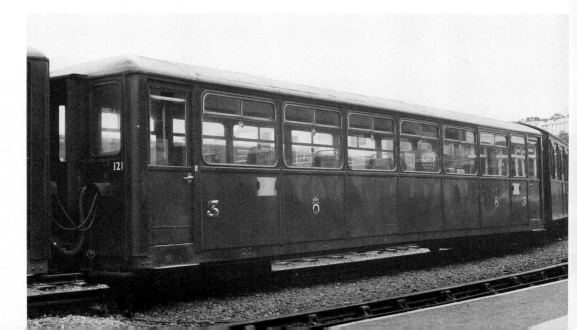

Push-Pull stock

Above:

The FR's first trial with push-pull working occurred in 1975, when it was decided to operate a shuttle service on the completed section of the deviation at Dduallt. For this purpose *Moel Hebog* was brought into use, along with a new coach, No 110. This coach was built for the shuttle in 1975 and was the prototype for the later steel bodied stock, although it did have a Boston Lodge-built underframe. The Porthmadog-end vestibule was fitted with a brake controller which could be operated by the guard when running downhill, control of the locomotive still remaining with its driver. When the ensemble were first required for traffic they ran in an unfinished state, windowless, doorless, and bonnetless, as shown. The occasion was a special for the Deviationists, prior to the first public working on 26 May 1975. *R. W. Miller*

Above left:

The latest incarnation of push-pull working on the FR first saw the light of day with the introduction of car No 111 to traffic in 1990. No 111 is a true driving trailer and its driver has full control over the locomotive at the far end of the train. The push-pull set will consist of Nos 111, 117 and 121, together with Carnforth-bodied Nos 112/4; the full concept of this stock is described in the text. The picture shows a three-car push-pull set, with *Conway Castle* bringing up the rear, at Minffordd on 7 May 1990. *Author*

Left:

The first of the Carnforth-built push-pull cars to enter service was No 112, seen here at Porthmadog on 13 July 1991. The underframes and bogies were built at Boston Lodge and finishing and fitting out were undertaken there. The doors are wide enough to take a wheelchair. *Author*

smoother ride. The net result is a comfortable vehicle about 2 tons tare (20%) lighter.

The self-steering bogie design, done in 1985/86, had the primary objective of reducing maintenance costs, especially wheel turning, a big factor on the line's tortuous route. The secondary objective was to improve ride quality and reduce noise. Major parameters for the new design were laid down as follows:

● Must be interchangeable with existing bogies;
● Wheelsets must be interchangeable with the extremely reliable roller bearing design of 1960;
● No metal-to-metal wearing contact;
● All brakegear must be simplified, compensated and bushed with proprietary components. Standard brake shoes to be used and accessible from underneath the vehicle;
● Short wheelbase to minimise angle of attack and, therefore, flangewear.

Two young students took on the challenge of the design of the primary suspension for their Mechanical Engineering course at Leeds University. Following fundamental work on wheel/rail interactions and the self-steering forces from conicity of the tread profile, they identified a Metalastik chevron orientation as suitable because, with a given vertical stiffness, the horizontal stiffness could be adjusted to allow self-steering. One possible problem was that low horizontal stiffness, to permit self-steering, might give rise to hunting of the wheelsets or even of the bogie. The first batch of bogies was fitted with conservatively high lateral stiffness. The second set was fitted with stiffness theoretically low enough for no flange contact to occur on the sharpest curve. So far there are no hunting problems and while it is too early to know the effect on flange wear, the railway is confident that it can expect an improvement because, as yet, there is no visible sign of wear, and by using video cameras it is clear that the bogies steer as predicted.

The railway has continued to use standard coil springs and hydraulic dampers for the secondary suspension but the steel-to-steel guide restraint for the top plank has been replaced by a rubber bushed horizontal arm. Standard FR Tufnol rubbing pads — bogie to body — and a Metalastik centre pivot bush have been adopted.

All this is a very far cry from the earliest FR passenger vehicles built to carry people on what many then thought was a dangerously narrow gauge. The old 'knife-board' carriage was the engineering solution of the day. Today known as 'Bug Boxes', these are extremely expensive to renovate because the timbers are carefully fashioned to match the original complex joints.

In 1872 Brown, Marshalls & Co built the first bogie passenger coaches (Nos 15 and 16) to go into regular service in Britain. In 1876 they built two more, Nos 17 and 18. These vehicles have been lovingly restored, with a quality of workmanship second to none. A superb outside finish has been achieved on No 17 by using materials not available to Brown, Marshalls, namely aluminium-bonded plywood with the aluminium on the outside. The intention, as always, is to improve quality and reduce maintenance; the paint finish on aluminium is more durable through absence of the movement there is with wood between wet and dry weather. It is too early to be certain of the long term results of this innovation.

(Based on a paper presented by David Pollock, General Manager 1983-1991, to the Institution of Mechanical Engineers on 5 November 1991.)

Left:
Car No 5 was entirely rebuilt by Ron Jarvis and returned to traffic in 1983. Car No 6 should return to use in 1992, following an extensive reconstruction, and work on overhauling Nos 3 and 4 is now in hand. Known on the railway as 'bug boxes', these cars are vacuum piped. No 5 was photographed on 16 June 1990.
Author

Welsh Highland Railway

In 1990 it became known that the Festiniog Railway Company had made a bid to purchase the trackbed of the old Welsh Highland Railway; the Welsh Highland Light Railway (1922) Ltd not having been liquidated, the trackbed was still in the hands of the Official Receiver. This bid, which caused more than a certain amount of controversy, did not meet with the approval of the Welsh Highland Light Railway (1964) Co; this company has established a base on the site of the standard gauge Beddgelert Siding at Porthmadog and has been working to gain access to the original WHR trackbed with Gwynedd County Council. The Festiniog's bid eventually became an attempt to lift the 1922 company out of receivership by Ffestiniog Railway (Holdings) Ltd, a subsidiary of the Festiniog Railway Trust. An application for this purpose, which also considered Gwynedd County Council's bid to buy the trackbed for £1.00 and the FR's original bid to buy it for £16,000, was made to the High Court. In a judgement given on 20 December 1991 the application to lift the Company out of receivership was turned down. The purchase bids were adjourned to allow the parties time for further talks. At the time of writing it is not known how the FR will proceed.

The Welsh Highland Railway connection
Above:
Welsh Highland single Fairlie *Moel Tryfan* came into FR ownership in 1937 and is seen in the Boston Lodge erecting shop. The photographer visited the FR on 8 July 1936. Except for the trailing bogie, later to provide pony truck wheelsets for *Linda* and *Blanche*, the remains of *Moel Tryfan* were cut up in 1954. *S. W. Baker*

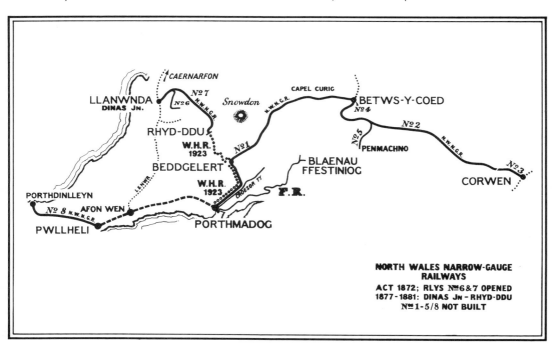

Below:
Welsh Highland relics in the FR archives, October 1991. The 'General Managers Office' plaque was fitted to the wall alongside the office door at Harbour station; a similar plaque for the FR was fitted on the opposite side of the door opening. The (blue) 'North Wales Narrow Gauge Ry' and 'Welsh Highland Railway' plates are enamel. *Author*

Bottom:
Boston Lodge locomotive shed interior in August 1936, with the Welsh Highland Railway's *Russell* hemmed in by Festiniog England locomotives, with *Prince* in front. In the foreground are the tanks and a power bogie from *James Spooner*, the latter showing great signs of wear where the driving wheel flanges have rubbed against the frame. *W. A. Camwell*

Bibliography

Beazley, Elisabeth; *Madocks and the Wonder of Wales*; Faber & Faber, 1967

Boyd, J. I. C.; *The Festiniog Railway*; Oakwood Press, 1975 (2 vols)

Boyd, J. I. C.; *Narrow Gauge Railways in South Caernarvonshire*, Oakwood Press, 1988/9 (2 vols)

City Press Services; *Blaenau Ffestiniog ... here we come!*; City Press Services, 1978

Festiniog Railway Co; *Traveller's Guide*; FR Co, 1990 edition

Garraway, A. G. W.; *Garraway Father and Son*; Middleton Press, 1985

Green, C. C.; *An Illustrated History of the Vale of Rheidol Light Railway*; Wild Swan Publications, 1986

Gurley, N. F.; *Narrow Gauge Steam out of Portmadoc - 25 years of the Festiniog Railway*; D. Bradford Barton, 1980

Hollingsworth, Brian; *Festiniog Adventure - The Festiniog Railway's Deviation Project*; David & Charles, 1981

Holliday & Edwards Ltd; *Croeso i Rheilffordd Festiniog/Welcome to the Festiniog Railway*; Holliday & Edwards Ltd, 1973

Isherwood, J. G.; *Slate - from Blaenau Ffestiniog*; AB Publishing, 1988

Jackson, Doug; *Rheilffordd Ffestiniog Railway ... the first 150 years*; FR Co, 1982

Johnson, Peter; *Railway World Special - The Welsh Narrow Gauge Railways*; Ian Allan, 1985, 2nd edition 1991

Johnson, Peter; *Festiniog 150: The History of the Ffestiniog Railway*; Ian Allan, 1986

Johnson, Peter (Ed); *Festiniog Railway Gravity Trains*; Festiniog Railway Heritage Group, 1986

Johnson, Peter; *Festiniog 150th Anniversary: A Celebration*; AB Publishing, 1987

Johnson, Peter; *Festiniog Railway Picture Postcards*; unpublished MS, 1991

Lewis, M. J. T.; *How Festiniog Got Its Railway*; Railway & Canal Historical Society, 2nd edition 1968

Lewis, M. J. T. (Ed); *The Slate Quarries of North Wales in 1873*; Snowdonia National Park Study Centre, 1987

Lewis, M. J. T. & Williams, M. C.; *Pioneers of Ffestiniog Slate*; Snowdonia National Park Study Centre, 1987

Lewis, M. J. T.; *Sails on the Dwyryd*; Snowdonia National Park Study Centre, 1989

Pollock, D.; *Preserved Railways - how to keep them going*; presented at the ordinary meeting of the Railway Division, Institution of Mechanical Engineers, 5 November 1991

'Taliesin'; *Festiniog Railway Locomotives*; AB Publishing, 1988

Vignes, Edouard (English translation by D. A. Boreham); *A Technical Study of the Festiniog & Other Narrow-Gauge Railways 1878*; P. E. Waters & Associates, 1986

Weaver, Rodney; 'Double Fairlie Celebration'; *Railway World*, January 1980

Whitehouse, P. B.; *Festiniog Railway Revival*; Ian Allan, 1963

Winton, John; *The Little Wonder - The Story of the Festiniog Railway*; Michael Joseph, 1986

Left:
Earl of Merioneth bursts out of the new Moelwyn Tunnel before the cosmetic stone portals were fitted. *FR Co*

Parliamentary Powers

The following acts and orders govern the operation of the Festiniog Railway:

● Act of Parliament 1832 (2/3 William IV Cap xlviii, for making and maintaining a railway or tramroad);
● Act of Parliament 1838 (1/2 Victoria Cap lxxx, for granting extra powers);
● Act of Parliament 1869 (32/33 Victoria Cap cxli, for widening and improving the railway and to raise further money and for other purposes);
● Act of Parliament 1892 (55/56 Victoria Cap xliv, for defining the scale of maximum rates and charges applicable);
● The Festiniog Railway (Light Railway) Order 1923 (Statutory Rules and Orders 1923/301, giving power to operate the railway authorised by Acts of 1832, 1838 and 1869 (railway No 1) as a light railway, to build the link line (railway no 2) to the Welsh Highland Railway, and for other purposes);
● North Wales Hydro-Electric Act, 1955;
● The Festiniog Railway (Light Railway) (Amendment) Order 1968 (Statutory Instrument 1968/178, power to construct railway No 3, the deviation line between Dduallt and Brookes Quarry);
● The Festiniog Railway (Light Railway) (Amendment) Order 1975 (Statutory Instrument 1975/1014, power to construct railway No 4, the deviation line between a junction with railway No 3, near Gelliwiog, and Tanygrisiau, and to abandon part of railway No 3 from the junction with railway No 4 and Brookes Quarry);
● The Blaenau Ffestiniog (Central Station) Light Railway Order 1981 (Statutory Instrument 1981/62, power to build the railway into the Central Station site, covers both standard and narrow gauge);
● The Festiniog Railway (Light Railway) (Amendment) Order 1982 (Statutory Instrument 1982/1456, concerning the Stwlan Dam Access Road and Glan-y-pwll level crossings);
● The Festiniog Railway (Light Railway) (Abandonment) Order, 4 March 1991 (Releasing the Company from 'any obligation to maintain and operate that length of the former route from a point immediately to the north of Dduallt Station for a distance of 28 chains in a northerly direction');
● The Festiniog Railway Quarry Lane, Minffordd Level Crossing Order 1986 (Made 13 June 1986, under section 1 of the Level Crossings Act 1983, to authorise conversion to an open level crossing).

Left:
Taliesin runs round its train at Tan-Y-bwlch in September 1958; the first season of operating to that point. The scene has changed somewhat over the intervening decades.